theatre & photography

Theatre &
Series Editors: Jen Harvie and Dan Rebellato

Theatre&
Series Standing Order ISBN 978–0–230–20327–3

You can receive future titles in this series as they are published by placing a standing order. Please contact your bookseller or, in case of difficulty, write to us at the address below with your name and address, the title of the series and the ISBN quoted above.

Customer Services Department, Macmillan Distribution Ltd, Houndmills, Basingstoke, Hampshire, RG21 6XS, UK

theatre &
photography

Joel Anderson

 macmillan international HIGHER EDUCATION

 RED GLOBE PRESS

First published 2015 by
RED GLOBE PRESS

Red Globe Press in the UK is an imprint of Springer Nature Limited,
registered in England, company number 785998, of 4 Crinan Street,
London, N1 9XW.

Red Globe Press® is a registered trademark in the United States,
the United Kingdom, Europe and other countries.

ISBN 978–0–230–27671–0   ISBN 978–1–137–34562–2 (eBook)

A catalogue record for this book is available from the British Library.

A catalog record for this book is available from the Library of Congress.

contents

series editors' preface

The theatre is everywhere, from entertainment districts to the fringes, from the rituals of government to the ceremony of the courtroom, from the spectacle of the sporting arena to the theatres of war. Across these many forms stretches a theatrical continuum through which cultures both assert and question themselves.

Theatre has been around for thousands of years, and the ways we study it have changed decisively. It's no longer enough to limit our attention to the canon of Western dramatic literature. Theatre has taken its place within a broad spectrum of performance, connecting it with the wider forces of ritual and revolt that thread through so many spheres of human culture. In turn, this has helped make connections across disciplines; over the past fifty years, theatre and performance have been deployed as key metaphors and practices with which to rethink gender, economics, war, language, the fine arts, culture and one's sense of self.

Theatre & is a long series of short books which hopes to capture the restless interdisciplinary energy of theatre and performance. Each book explores connections between theatre and some aspect of the wider world, asking how the theatre might illuminate the world and how the world might illuminate the theatre. Each book is written by a leading theatre scholar and represents the cutting edge of critical thinking in the discipline.

We have been mindful, however, that the philosophical and theoretical complexity of much contemporary academic writing can act as a barrier to a wider readership. A key aim for these books is that they should all be readable in one sitting by anyone with a curiosity about the subject. The books are challenging, pugnacious, visionary sometimes and, above all, clear. We hope you enjoy them.

Jen Harvie and Dan Rebellato

theatre & photography

T heatre is a picture; but it is a moving picture whose details one has not the time to
examine.

Denis Diderot,
Letter to Madame Riccoboni, 1758

The relationship between photography and theatre is at
once clear and obscure – the two appear quite distinct and
separate in terms of their operations and functioning: photography deals in still images, duplicated and circulated,
whereas theatre seems to be about motion, events experienced in a particular place with specific participants. Rather
than attempting to define first photography, and then theatre, or vice versa, and to determine the particularities of
each, this book shows how the two might provide stand-
points for comprehending each other, and considers the
interactions between photography and theatre as a strategy
for understanding both. The book privileges points at which

the two seem intertwined, and where two conceptions of the image, one initially appearing to belong to theatre, the other to photography, assert themselves: one kind of image is crafted, and creates meaning; the other reports reality or likeness.

The introductory section focuses on photography as constituent of a piece of street theatre by an unknown artist, introducing questions that emerge from one meeting of photography and theatre. This advances the idea that photography can tell us something about theatre, and theatre can tell us something about photography. The following parts of this book approach photography and theatre from different angles. Part One examines instances of photography, photographs, and photographing appearing in stage works, focusing on how photography has figured in plays. Part Two reframes the question, examining how theatre has been photographed. Part Three stages a collision between photography and theatre which is also that of the two kinds of image I suggest haunt this enquiry: the theories and practices of playwright, writer, and director Bertolt Brecht propose an uneasy synthesis between the two.

An unknown street performer: theatre of photography

In Edinburgh, during the Festival in 1996, walking alone along Grassmarket, I chanced upon some street theatre. A solo artist, a clown, was receiving applause for whatever feat he had just performed. The crowd was large, arranged in a circle several people deep. I stopped to watch as the performer began his next routine. With a single word, he asked for a volunteer, and the assembly at once displayed the visible discomfort one might expect in the face of a call for audience participation. There ensued moments of silence as each of us – I had joined the crowd by this point – rehearsed different strategies in response to this request: watching, looking away, never sure whether feigned aloofness or performed attention is the best way to ensure not ending up onstage. We smiled nervously, or did our best to look serious, knowing obvious reluctance might well, in such a situation, be exactly what this kind of performer seeks from potential victims. The discomfort was of course intensified by the fact that this was happening to us not in a theatre, but in a public street, and this arena opened up the possibility that anything we might end up doing onstage would be in plain sight of not just the group (currently enjoying momentary solidarity in the face of being asked to participate), but potentially anybody passing by. The silence started to feel long; it was uncomfortable but expectant (perhaps like the silence of the crowd at the public gibbet that had stood at Grassmarket centuries earlier). The clown turned on the spot, seeking eye contact. We still had no idea what the participant might have to do as part of the contract that would be created once somebody stepped onstage, and this galvanised our reluctance, even turning it into a sense of righteous indignation: we needed more information. The clown clarified his request with two words: he wanted 'a child'. Some in the crowd seemed relieved, perhaps since children are surely – given their position in society – fair game for this kind of thing (whatever this kind of thing is): the stakes are lower, since their potential embarrassment onstage is a less serious affair than the public shaming of an adult; indeed, children are surely meant to display the enthusiasm that helps make audience participation so troubling.

Eventually, a child came forward, or rather was offered up by his father. The boy dutifully made his way from the crowd to the stage area, where the clown positioned him dead centre, then continued to manipulate him, sculpting his body into position, guiding his arm and hand into a 'thumbs-up' sign. Then the clown turned again towards the crowd, and asked for another one, another child. He turned to the other side of the circle. He was seeking to recruit again, and specified with a word that he wanted a girl this time. There was some further relief, since the game was now perhaps discernible – some children would be placed in the middle of a circle of spectators. A girl bounded forward, seemingly keen to take part. She was positioned next to the boy, and – standing facing her – the clown mimed that she should smile, resulting in a frozen grimace on the girl's face.

This formed a tableau, which was clearly facing in one direction, and some members of the crowd shuffled around to the optimum viewing position, facing the two children; a few stayed in their place but, perhaps when they found themselves under the gaze of the mass, eventually moved around to join the others. The clown, who throughout spoke only a couple of words at a time, now called for 'Mum!' Silence. He selected a woman, perhaps at random, or perhaps because she made too much, or too little, eye contact, or smiled, or did whatever it is that suggests 'volunteer' to a clown. She was manoeuvred to stand behind the children, and her hand was placed atop the girl's head. Quickly now, the clown looked around the circle again. 'Dad?' He made his selection, and a man (who, I recall, very formally shook the clown's hand later, when the routine was over) was positioned with his arm around the woman, behind the children. He had an SLR camera around his neck on a wide strap. The tableau had expanded to incorporate this new element, and our view widened to take it in. I started to understand something of the routine: an image of a 'nuclear family' was being constituted onstage – Mum, Dad, and the Kids. The clown stepped back to admire his sculpture, tilting his head and squinting, mimicking the gestures of an artist scrutinising a work in progress. He made a rectangle with his fingers, like film directors do (or at least like they do in films), then turned this apparatus on the crowd; the spectators were no longer in a circle, but were all clustered where he now stood viewing them (with passers-by even avoiding the frontality of the 'stage' side). Having stopped his roving rectangle upon one section of the crowd, he zoomed in, and without voicing a request this time, reached out both arms and gently pulled an elderly woman from the front row, turning her around on the spot with a flourish and introducing her: 'Granny!' She was placed next to 'Dad' and, without needing to be sculpted much at all, assumed an appropriate pose.

The next request was of a different order: the clown asked for a 'camera', which was provided by somebody to

the side of the huddled crowd, who strode into the performing area and helpfully pointed out the position of the
shutter button as he handed the clown his 35 mm compact.
After a moment of testing different angles, making a show
of the skill and precision required for the task at hand, the
clown took a single flash photograph of this constructed family, then bowed, camera in hand, before returning it to its
owner, who was also then encouraged to come onstage and
take a bow. Applause. The 'family' relaxed for a moment,
and performed an uncertain and disorganised curtain call,
but then snappily resumed their pose when members of
the crowd took their cue from the clown's photographing
and started to take their own pictures of the tableau. This
held for some time, with the clown even, at the request of
the paparazzi-like chorus, joining the family, lying at their
feet, or gesturing towards them. Photographers craned and
crouched, some attempting a low-angle shot incorporating
the historical buildings of the street in the frame, possibly
in some cases even managing to get the castle in the background, until the clown started his next routine.

The performance's final moments – with people photographing using an array of different cameras, taking various
approaches to the task, and making, consciously or not, the
same gestures the clown had aped seconds earlier – reveal
part of the conceit that made this piece function at all. From
uneasy beginnings, everybody watching ultimately recognised the final tableau of the show, arrived at progressively
via a few unnerving moments of audience participation. It
was a conventional photographic pose, and the later entrants

to the scene showed their recognition by posing appropriately (albeit with embarrassment), as did the spectators when they took up their own cameras. The clown performance called upon, but also made strange, the habitual act of photographing. It placed the process of the creation of a posed photograph onstage; the frozen image was in no way surprising in itself, but was held for a great deal longer than is usual. Like any successful street theatre perhaps, this performance breached (albeit gently) established codes and contracts of civic living simply by inviting people to stop. Shuffling motion and uncertain, wavering stillness thus took up a place in streets normally serving to enable motion between points, getting from A to B, and – this being Edinburgh, and during the Festival – touristic photographing; one reason people stop in the street (to photograph or be photographed) was incorporated into a demonstration of that act's own absurdity. The piece began to make sense with the introduction of photography, and teased the conventions of touristic and family photographs.

After all, there is nothing more ordinary, especially given the context, than people photographing family and friends, posing for a group shot. Indeed, photographing family and friends in the street is established enough to enjoy a set of entitlements, permitted even to disrupt the flow of traffic. In some cities, and especially around tourist sites, passers-by will take detours or stop and wait to avoid getting between photographer and photographed, perhaps because of the risk both of ruining a picture (more important perhaps with film photography, when every exposure carries a tangible cost) and of ending up in the picture (if only as a blurry foreign object). The contemporary 'selfie' (made considerably easier with front-facing mobile phone cameras) is perhaps changing things, but the recruitment of passers-by to take photographs of a group, a couple, or occasionally even an individual remains a common occurrence in most places where there are tourists, especially in the foreground of some significant site. A scene in the comedy *Curb Your Enthusiasm* (HBO, series 4, 2004) plays (as often in *Curb*) on the fragility of the social contract. The protagonist, Larry, is asked to photograph a holidaying couple, a man and a woman, but, upon taking the camera and preparing to take the shot, he finds himself excessively directed by the man: Larry thinks the picture will be better if shot portrait (with the camera on its side), whereas the camera's owner favours landscape (he states that he might render the shot portrait by way of Photoshop, but wants to keep his options open). Larry points out that he is the one who can see what the shot will look like, insisting on his autonomy as designated photographer; when the woman sides with him, it prompts a couple-fight. At this point, Larry hands back the camera, much to the consternation of the man, who sees this breach of the rules as warranting an attempt to jinx Larry's stage performance taking place that night.

In the clown performance, photographic posing in a touristic mode was placed onstage, mapping for a time a camera's viewpoint onto that of the audience, who accepted this by shifting to face the image head-on, seeming to zoom in on the subject. Writing in the early 1960s, Marshall

McLuhan described in his book *Understanding Media* (1964) the central role of the camera in the development of what he called 'the new tourism'. McLuhan claimed that photography – in conjunction with faster modes of displacement, and particularly commercial airlines – had effectively reversed what travel had previously been, meaning that the figure of the traveller as intrepid explorer became obsolete, since travel could no longer be about the discovery of new sights and sites. However remote the destination, McLuhan suggested, the new tourist did not travel into the unknown, but rather went forth to verify scenes already seen in photographs, checking them against the existing pictures and creating a personal version. (McLuhan made this point fifty years ago; the shift he described has continued apace with subsequent developments in air travel and photographic media and distribution.) The photographer stalks and quests in order to mark presence; in a contemporary context, one might suggest that touristic photography thus seeks the condition of the selfie.

Such an understanding of photography might not be limited to touristic photographing; rather, touristic photography might merely expose a larger discourse. Vilém Flusser, in his *Towards a Philosophy of Photography* (2000), presents the striking idea that each photograph taken reduces the number of possible photographs by one, like game being bagged, or sights being ticked off a real or imaginary list of must-sees (in the clown performance, even a tableau mocking touristic photographing itself became a subject for photography). Susan Sontag describes, in her 1977 book *On*

Photography, one of the first theoretical books on the subject published in English, how the camera had replaced the gun on safaris, with the quest for the perfect shot replacing the quest for an actual trophy (p. 11). Writing about how – with the advent of portable cameras – photographers became part of the fabric of the modern city, Sontag describes the photographer deep in the task of stitching together the city's sights by way of aleatory walks: 'reconnoitering, stalking, cruising the urban inferno, the voyeuristic stroller who discovers the city as a landscape of voluptuous extremes' (p. 43). Sontag describes this figure, moving through the streets, part of the crowd but retaining a crucial distance, as an updated – and armed – version of the *flâneur* (p. 43), the solitary, roving pedestrian invoked by Edgar Allan Poe and Charles Baudelaire in the nineteenth century. He (most *flâneurs* do seem to be men in these early accounts) roams and sleuths, taking in the spectacle the city has to offer, making sense, by way of constant watching and ceaseless motion, of its new age of industrial capitalism.

A *flâneur*/photographer becomes part of the spectacle, just as photographing itself ended up in the picture in the clown performance. Just as the family was sculpted into an archetypal pose, with the body positions and expressions seeming, as the piece and the pose went on, ever more ridic-ulous, the gestures of the clown-as-photographer/director were heightened and parodic. The clown approached the task (as clowns will) with great seriousness, seeking to embody, by way of emulating the outward features of the practice, the figure of the great photographer, possessor of technical abilities and artistic sensibilities This exposed the ridiculousness of gestures of photographing, and it revealed how this task, although in its essence little more than pushing a button, might sometimes demand concentration (echoed in the poses of the audience members when they took their turn to photograph). Photographer Martine Franck (who was a street photographer and also a theatre photographer, notably at the Théâtre du Soleil in France), in a book of her photographs entitled *One Day to the Next* (1998), described how photographic concentration is potentially a serious matter: in seeking to capture a subject, the photographer becomes solipsistic, spatially unaware, ignorant of the space outside the frame, and the quest for an image may become dangerous: 'for a split second nothing else exists outside the frame, and to get the right frame one is constantly moving forwards, backwards, to the side' (p. 10). Franck described how her own grandfather died by falling backwards off an Ostend dike while composing a shot.

Family photographs must make up a significant proportion of all photographic images taken over the more than one hundred and fifty years since the invention of photography. Sontag pays attention to the family photograph in her book in terms of the spectacle of the family equipped for photography, with the designated photographer wearing a camera on any given family trip: cameras 'go with family life' (*On Photography*, p. 5). Pierre Bourdieu, in his *Photography: A Middle-Brow Art*, published in France in 1965, writes about the widened uses of photography, identifying its 'family function': that of 'solemnizing and immortalizing the high points of family life, in short, of reinforcing the integration of the family group by reasserting the sense that it has both of itself and of its unity' (p. 19). This point is taken up by another major photography critic, Rosalind Krauss, who, in 'A Note on Photography and the Simulacral' (1984), suggests that 'the camera is an agent in the collective fantasy of family cohesion, and in that sense the camera is a projective tool, part of the theatre that the family constructs to convince itself that it is together and whole' (p. 56). Sontag sees family photographs forming a body of images that, unlike the impersonal and exhaustive archives in which pictures might institutionally be stocked and stored, 'bears witness to its connectedness' (p. 5). This idea is present too in a 1980 essay entitled 'Uses of Photography', a response to Sontag's book. In this essay, John Berger makes a distinction between 'public' and 'private' uses of photographs, and suggests that family photography resides in the private. For Berger, a private photograph is 'appreciated and read in a context which is continuous with that from which the camera removed it' (p. 55), whereas a public photograph 'usually presents an event, a seized set of appearances, which has nothing to do with us, its readers or with the original meaning of the event' (p. 56). Berger suggests that contextualisation and 'connectedness' is what nourishes private photographs, keeping them alive, whereas the public photograph 'is torn from its context, and becomes a dead object which, exactly because it is dead, lends itself to any arbitrary use' (p. 60). And there are consequences to its being used: much photography participates, according to Berger, in the construction of a dehumanising worldview, privileging distance and division. Berger suggests that a different approach, bringing to bear on all photographs the kind of use normally reserved for private photographs, might impact the possibilities of the very idea of the public. For Berger, a use of photographs from beyond our strict family contexts, encompassing the full range of human experience but managing to retain the principle of collectivity applied to the family photograph, might foster links between people, challenging the everyday experience of alienation. Berger, critical of the title and project of an ambitious and highly controversial exhibition and book from 1955, *The Family of Man* (described in the prologue by Carl Sandburg as 'A camera testament, a drama of the grand canyon of humanity, an epic woven of fun, mystery and holiness', p. 3), suggests that photography holds the power to create such a family, although this power remains largely unexploited.

The Edinburgh street performance staged something along the lines of the process Berger proposes: by blurring distinctions between private and public, and by staging a family photograph not informed by family ties, it disrupted the experience of alienation as encountered in a city crowd. The clown cast a false family, constituted more or less at random: a few individuals were temporarily displaced from the context of their own families and entourages, as they were from their position as spectators. By way of a merging of photography and theatre, the show, at its conclusion, created this stage 'family' as something both ridiculous and at the same time believable. Indeed, as it slowly emerged that this was a family portrait, it became almost impossible not to seek, and then to find, family resemblances among the individuals, to cast them and connect them in the mind as a coherent and contiguous group. By way of staging, a connectedness formed over a few uncomfortable and slow minutes, although it did not endure much longer than the click of the camera.

In addition to this photographic held pose, and the theatrical act of photographing that formed the final conceit of the piece, a material photograph also surely resulted from the concluding click. Or, rather, a latently material photograph, since the camera used was a film camera. Film photography, one mode of 'chemical' photography, makes particular demands in terms of time: unlike digital cameras, most of which allow for the image to be viewed (and, increasingly, shared) almost instantaneously (and such a possibility might nuance the performance if attempted today), analogue cameras use film, which has to be processed, and the resulting image printed onto paper. In 1996, this would have entailed a wait of an hour or so at the very least (some chemists and labs offered a one-hour service) – or more usually several days, since film was typically dropped off at or posted to a lab for processing and printing. Film photography is also contingent – we cannot know whether the image taken was ever printed (or whether it even 'came out'; indeed, we cannot know whether the camera was actually loaded), but the image likely sits today in a set of twenty-four or thirty-six images, perhaps alongside other, more conventional, photographs of tourist sites or members of the photographer's family on a day out in Edinburgh. John Szarkowski suggested in his 1966 work *The Photographer's Eye* that to 'quote out of context is the essence of the photographer's craft' (p. 70). The performance summoned photography's discontinuity, as characterised by the film strip, perhaps to posit the possibility of connectedness.

The clown performance brought theatre and photography together, staging photographing and photographing staging; the act of constructing a pose, and then the act of photographing, took centre stage; the piece ended with a snapshot, leaving behind a photograph, which, although not visible, was crucial within the dramaturgy of the piece. The photograph, both the unseen material image and the stage 'photograph' made of the stilled bodies, was staged (into an image of a family), and it was the retroactive justification for the action that preceded it. The performance pitched photography's stillness against theatre's assembling of a scene, the capturing of an event against the creation of an image. And, bringing photography and theatre together, it arranged and exposed their connections.

part one: photography onstage

Numerous plays feature photographers, photography, or photographs. Here, the focus is on plays where photography has a particular significance, resonating with – or against – the work in which it takes place. Often, the union of photography and theatre on the page or onstage provides a vantage point from which theatre itself might be examined. While a discussion of photography onstage might immediately bring to mind the projection of photographic images onto a backdrop or screen, this is not specifically addressed here (with the exception of the last example, where such practice forms part of a much larger photographic discourse and where it is explicit in the stage directions); in part, this is because the question of projections onstage has been explored in some depth (notably in Béatrice Picon-Vallin's 1998 collection entitled *Les Écrans sur la scène*). Moreover, the use of projections in the theatre, although clearly linked to photography and photographic technology, involves a wide range of kinds of projection – from what is considered to be its earliest recruitment, with the use of drawings, text, and moving images by the director and producer Erwin Piscator (1893–1966) in Germany in the 1920s, to the more recent use of video technology to project photographs and video clips – and it would be necessary to determine how the photographic projections are distinct from moving ones. Instead, the focus is on photography figuring as an element of the drama.

Examples of photography in drama date back to the very early days of photography, and it would not be possible to list every instance; photography is one of the many ordinary or extraordinary activities that might figure in the plot of a play. Notable photographers appearing in plays, not examined in depth here, include the unnamed photographer in Noël Coward's *Design for Living* (Ethel Barrymore Theatre, New York City, 1933), who accompanies Mr Birbeck from the *Evening Standard* to photograph Leo, a playwright who has recently found success. The press photograph is emblematic here of the 'grotesque' spectacle of celebrity, of which Leo is a recent victim: Act 1, Scene 1 ends with the tableau of an enraged Leo coaxed into holding a smile for the camera, posing in front of his desk. A more recent example of photography occupying a significant role in a play can be found in Timberlake Wertenbaker's *The Line* (Arcola, London, 2009), a biographical work about Edgar Degas (1834–1917) staging the influence of photography on the artist's work ('A photographer is like a fisherman, netting the moment', p. 32).

Photography in a play can, as will be considered in this part, be emblematic of truth, of objective reality, and can constitute hard evidence. But it can also, even by way of encompassing such usages, stand for fakery, fabrication, or the manipulation and rearrangement of truth. Photographs are sometimes recruited onstage as bearers of truth because they seem to resist the influence of prior knowledge, of circumstance, of context, and sometimes they are interjected, out of context, into a situation; such complex effects of photography are apparent when it confronts theatre's capacity to make things viewable, to exclude and include.

The mirror of nature: *The Octoroon*

An early example of photography featuring in a play, and surely the first in which photography occupies a key position in the plot, is Dion Boucicault's melodrama *The Octoroon* (Winter Garden Theatre, New York, 1859). The play was adapted from a novel entitled *The Quadroon* (the word 'octoroon' is an obsolete term for somebody who is 'one-eighth black'). A single photograph is central to the piece. Whereas in the clown performance recounted in the previous section, the photograph was invisible and latent, *The Octoroon* stages the (accidental) taking of a photograph, and has as its dramatic high point the appearance of the resulting image onstage. The play concerns the machinations of a family fighting over ownership of a Louisiana plantation and its slaves. It is set on a plantation previously owned by Judge Peyton, who has died, financially ruined, two years earlier. George Peyton, the Judge's nephew, arrives from Paris at the property he has inherited. He falls in love with Zoe, Judge Peyton's daughter and the octoroon of the play's title. Property relations are a theme of the play, and are focused on and exposed through Zoe: as an octoroon, she enjoys a complicated status within two legal structures – marriage (George cannot marry Zoe because of her origins, since mixed marriages are not lawful) and inheritance (she, along with the slaves, can be put up for auction with the plantation estate).

The conflicts of the play culminate in a murder. Jacob M'Closky, the plantation overseer, plans to take over the plantation and, by extension, to take ownership of Zoe. M'Closky's plan depends upon the ruin of Mrs Peyton, the late Judge's wife. In order to prevent delivery of a banker's draft arriving from Liverpool that would enable Mrs Peyton to keep the property, M'Closky murders Paul, the slave who is carrying it. There are no witnesses. Just before the murder, Paul has loaded a photographic plate into Salem Scudder's old and unreliable camera (copying the technical actions he has seen Scudder undertake many times), the large device having been left behind by Scudder following a session of portraiture. Paul does this during some horseplay with an 'Indian', Wahnotee (who fears for his life, thinking the camera is a gun). The camera is still in place during the murder. Afterwards, when M'Closky has left the scene, Wahnotee re-enters and, seeing Paul dead near the camera, smashes it with his tomahawk.

Wahnotee is accused of Paul's murder, and is to be lynched for this crime, a quasi-tribunal having been set up in haste. Scudder's broken 'photographic apparatus' is initially presented as evidence, contributing to the set of exhibits against Wahnotee, along with bloodstains and a half-empty rum bottle. But, during the course of the trial, Pete, another slave, points out that the broken camera, which he calls a 'telescope machine' (p. 82), has a picture sticking out of it. It turns out that the camera was triggered by Paul just before his own murder, and the photographic plate shows M'Closky, immobile as he reads the banker's draft he has intercepted, standing over Paul's body, tomahawk in hand. This constitutes proof positive of Wahnotee's innocence and of M'Closky's guilt, and M'Closky is put on trial, with the photographic plate as evidence, or even – as the camera's owner Scudder puts it – constituting the case against him, taking the stand as a witness: 'your accuser is that picter of the crime' (p. 83). The broken camera is anthropomorphised, delivering with its image something akin to deathbed testimony, a form of evidence (usually called a 'dying declaration' in the US legal system) based on the principle of *Nemo moriturus praesumitur mentiri* (a Latin maxim meaning that the dying are presumed to speak the truth); such evidence is often admissible where the same evidence given by somebody not on their deathbed would be dismissed as hearsay.

Scudder, it is revealed earlier in the play, was formerly a travelling photographer, and he pronounces on photography's power to reveal, stating that 'the machine can't err' (p. 14), and later, 'the apparatus can't lie' (p. 82). Drawing on his experience of making portraits, he suggests that the likeness provided by a photograph is always true, even when that truth is, as it often will be, unpalatable or unexpected – the camera sees the sitter more clearly than the sitter does. The photograph's direct presence at the events and its rendering of truth place it above the rest of the assembly; the evidence on a photographic plate is stronger than verbal testimony, and this notion that it cannot be challenged is here reinforced by the fact that no human – at least deliberately – operated the camera that made the incriminating image (Paul is actually trying to take his own 'likeness' as he imitates Scudder's gestures for setting up the machine). Through a misfire, through the limited expertise of Paul, the camera functions as if of its own accord – the image effectively making itself (indeed, we must also assume that the photographic plate developed itself, as there is no mention of it having been processed; the image appears to emerge from the camera fully formed, which adds to the supernatural or spiritual import of the event). This corresponds to a certain conception of photography contemporary with the play: Susan Sontag states that 'The earliest photographers talked as if the camera were a copying machine; as if, while people operate cameras, it is the camera that sees' (*On Photography*, p. 67).

The plot device whereby a sudden and unexpected event resolves an apparently impossible situation, usually at the end of a play and often with a new character's arrival, is called *deus ex machina* (Latin for 'god from the machine', and referring originally to stage machinery – a crane device or a trapdoor from which a figure might appear in ancient

theatre). In *The Octoroon*, justice and resolution in the last
act also come via a mechanical device. And this is described
in spiritual terms: when the photographic plate is presented, with Pete illuminating it with a lantern, Scudder
refers to the process by which light impacts upon the photosensitive materials as if the light were divine: 'The Eye of
the Eternal was on you – the blessed sun in heaven, that,
looking down, struck upon this plate the image of the deed'
(p. 83). This corresponds to a notion from an early text on
photography by Oliver Wendell Holmes, 'The Stereoscope
and the Stereograph', published in 1859, the same year as
the first production of *The Octoroon*: that photography (he is
specifically discussing the Daguerreotype – the first mass-
produced system of plate photography, dating from 1839)
has become so commonplace that we forget its 'miraculous
nature, as we forget that of the sun itself, to which we owe
the creations of our new art' (p. 73). Holmes seems to propose the sun as the author of the photograph, in the same
essay giving an oft-quoted description of photography: 'the
mirror with a memory' (p. 74). In another early text on the
subject of 'Photography', published two years earlier, Lady
Elizabeth Eastlake calls photographers 'the sun's votaries'
(p. 41), and her essay, an account of the technical history of
photography and consideration of the relationship between
the mechanical images of photography and art, hinges upon
'how far the sun may be considered an artist' (p. 43).

In a play that explores the law's relationship to the state,
the photographic plate is presented as incontestable (and
ultimately victorious) truth, recalling Moses' table of laws,

etched by God Himself. This play of light and dark, and the black and white of photography, channels and amplifies the racial politics of the play, and points to the legal 'grey area' constituted by the title character, and to questions around visibility and representation, or representability (the photographic plate is effectively the prosecution). Photography, in the play, offers the possibility of truth beyond appearances and social status, beyond the lies and deceit of characters, and beyond subjective or interested positions. All of this participates too in the interplay of theatre and photography in the play. Both set up the possibility of seeing, both are copies, and both can be mechanisms for retrieving memory and determining truth. But photography is shown to expose, as well as transcend, the errors and corruption of mortals, with theatre itself taking the stage in the form of a mock-trial, always already a theatrical setup.

The play points towards a more just and fair future, and the new technology of photography embodies this possibility. Photography, the carrier of evidence, is presented in an optimistic light, with new powers of truth-telling (or truth-rendering at least) seeming to signal the end of an old and corrupt system, and an emerging enlightened age (there are in fact two versions of the play: in the version presented in Britain, but not that presented in America, Zoe and George marry). But the evidentiary potential of the nascent practice of photography has not always been characterised so positively or as a vector of emancipation. When the play was written, photography had been recognised as a device for producing evidence, and this had already led to institutional and oppressive usages; John Tagg, in his 1988 book *The Burden of Representation*, states that as early as the 1840s, police forces were employing civilian photographers (pp. 74–75). Sontag discusses the camera's ability to incriminate and dominate:

> photographs became a useful tool of modern states in the surveillance and control of their increasingly mobile populations. In another version of its utility, the camera record justifies. A photograph passes for incontrovertible proof that a given thing happened. The picture may distort; but there is always a presumption that something exists, or did exist, which is like what's in the picture. (*On Photography*, p. 3)

Sontag suggests that the starting point of this kind of usage was the suppression of the Paris Communards in June 1871, positing photography as something potentially rather more negative and reactionary than does the play.

The unseen photograph: *An Inspector Calls*

The device of the revelatory photograph in drama is familiar to the point of being a cliché (which incidentally is the French term for a 'snapshot'), and is of course the stuff of the courtroom drama, wherein a photograph can serve as a pivotal piece of evidence. But the photograph's reputation for truth is often such that, paradoxically, no burden is placed on its content – its presence on the stage or on the stand might be enough. It is such an idea that shapes the role of a photograph in J. B. Priestley's *An Inspector Calls* (Kamerny Theatre/Leningrad Theatre Company, Moscow, 1945).

An Inspector Calls, like *The Octoroon*, involves a quasi-judicial setup, and also concerns the question of responsibility for the death of an individual. But no photographing takes place as part of the play's plot. Rather, it is an old photograph of the deceased, and not of a crime, that prompts much of the action as we learn a long and complex history of the assembled characters and their relationships with the photographed dead woman. The photograph is used like a piece of evidence, introduced into the situation, serving as an *aide-memoire* and a challenge to the characters. The audience never actually sees the photograph, only the effect it has on the play's characters when they individually view it.

Inspector Goole arrives unexpectedly at the Birling household, where Arthur Birling is hosting a dinner to celebrate the engagement of his daughter, Sheila, to Gerald Croft. The Inspector announces the suicide of a young woman, Eva Smith (but also known, it turns out, as Daisy Renton, and as Mrs Birling), and suggests, initially rather vaguely, that the diners might have some involvement in what has happened, or in the 'chain of events'. Mr Birling quite quickly recognises the young woman, acknowledging that she was an employee at his factory who was discharged more than eighteen months earlier for asking for a pay rise and for her part in a subsequent strike. Birling, under questioning from the Inspector, denies, however, having played any role in the young woman's death. The Inspector questions the others present, and each time exposes connections, some quite well hidden, between them and the deceased. All of them have, from a position of power over the woman, impacted her life and played a part in her fate, it turns out. The Inspector conducts a sustained and careful series of interrogations, establishing a complex case, extracting testimony from, and setting traps for, the powerful and confident characters he is visiting. A photograph he wields of the young woman is crucial to his strategy. Just as the audience does not see the image, the Inspector is careful to restrict how and when it is seen by each character:

> **Gerald**: [showing annoyance]: Any particular reason why I shouldn't see this girl's photo-graph, Inspector?
> **Inspector**: [coolly, looking hard at him]: There might be.
> **Eric**: And the same applies to me, I suppose?
> **Inspector**: Yes. (pp. 170–71)

The Inspector relies upon the effect the photograph will have on each to provide a mechanism by which they might potentially incriminate themselves. In the quasi-judicial situation, the photograph's effectiveness stems from its ability to posit incontestable likeness. In the absence of material proof, the Inspector must rely on confession, on reactions to his challenges, and particularly on reactions to the sight of the photograph, itself amounting to an accusation meriting a response. The Inspector controls the circulation of the image ('It's the way I like to go to work. One person and one line of inquiry at a time', p. 171) because each of the interrogated characters has known the dead woman in different circumstances (and even under different names), all of which he must bring together in establishing what has happened. The photograph in each case is a spur to memory, and the impetus for an admission of guilt. The photograph serves for the Inspector as a rhetorical device. When the Inspector has exited, towards the end of the play, without revealing any clear consequence of his investigation, the characters begin to question the veracity of his claims, and even consider how they might have been manipulated by the use of the photograph. Each character's recognition of the girl in the image has been key to the Inspector's case, and they recall the care with which he employed it. They conclude that he might have performed a kind of conjurer's trick, actually showing different photographs to different characters, a bluff undertaken in order to push the characters into testimony, and they are aware that his strategy might well have worked. The characters' suggestion that there might have been more than one photograph echoes the fact that the dead woman was known by three different names, and furthermore points to the way in which, in subordinate roles (as employee, as charity case, and in the unofficial post of Gerald's mistress), she has been interchangeable. The photograph has effectively brought the characters face to face with the woman they have known, by whatever name, even if the name is sometimes not initially recalled. A denial of the particularity of this individual, of the specificity of the relationship, is each character's rationalisation and attempt to deny responsibility for the suicide; they protest they have done nothing out of malice towards this woman. But the Inspector successfully shows how the young woman's fate must be understood as the result of an interwoven mass of decisions, a network of abuse at the hands of a societal system. None of the assembled dinner guests is actually directly culpable (although some have clearly behaved immorally); there has not been a murder, but an accusation of liability is levelled, aimed at the system each of the characters defends and services as a member of the ruling class: the employer is found to have played a part, but so is the employer's wife, representing civil society (which is shown to be arbitrary and moralistic, as well as repressive). The photograph gives a face to Eva/Daisy/Mrs Birling, oppressed and subject to the machinations of power, occupying a series of delineated roles.

The photograph is as mysterious and ephemeral as is the Inspector himself, who vanishes following the execution of the investigation, having extracted confessions and even an acknowledgement of systemic corruption and amorality: he may not have existed at all, but the case he makes persists, seeming to reassert itself in the concluding scene. The crime in this case is an abstract and a compound one, and the perpetrator an entire apparatus. As such there is no possible photograph that could show the crime or someone caught in the act; there is no vantage point from which the capitalist system, whose representatives reluctantly reveal their parts under scrutiny by the Inspector, can be viewed or photographed. Instead, the photograph makes its charges by standing as material evidence of the woman's having existed; the various roles and subservient capacities in which each has known her are consolidated in a face in a photograph. The appearance out of context of this likeness, in the house and on the stage, and the fact that it demands to be accepted as truthful prompt a dissolution of the assembled diners' carefully crafted appearance of decency and respectability around the family dinner table. Appearances are demonstrated to be deceptive; the fixed image persists as the falsehoods melt.

In two plays, then, a photograph is called upon to guarantee truth: in *The Octoroon*, it is the photograph as a representation, an index, which signals a hidden event and points the finger at the guilty party; in *An Inspector Calls*, it is the presence of a photographic likeness that counts, and that photograph attests only to the existence of the victim – it is harnessed rhetorically. Thus, in *The Octoroon*, the photograph is considered to be a faithful rendering of a moment, which needs little explanation – it speaks for itself, whereas in *An Inspector Calls*, the unseen photograph is brandished for maximum impact – it has no juridical or moral weight of its own, but gains this by way of how it – as a truth – can be used to prompt a response when presented or concealed, framed or staged, deftly angled towards or away from its viewers.

A play on photography: *The Wild Duck*

Photography plays a role in the symbolic stage universe in Henrik Ibsen's *The Wild Duck* (Den Nationale Scene, Bergen, Norway, 1885), activating the play's play on light and darkness, sight and blindness. In the play, photography is a double of theatre, a participant in the same economy of truth and appearance, and it is highlighted as a new representational modality and emerging professional practice. Any claim of realism courts analogies with the photographic, and there is a particularly strong relationship between photography and Ibsen, who reportedly considered becoming a photographer when uncertain of his future as a writer of poetry, and was urged in 1868 by Bjørnstjerne Bjørnson to become a playwright and thus produce 'comedy by photography' (as recounted in Thomas Herbert Dickinson's *An Outline of Contemporary Drama*, 1969, p. 76). *The Wild Duck* seems highly critical of photography; any idea that photography offers access to truth in the play is heavily nuanced, and counterbalanced by the figuring of photography as a professional craft and social practice, and, linked to this, by drawing attention to photography's capacity to manipulate and falsify.

The play features a professional photographer, Hjalmar Ekdal, and exposes from the start this relatively new profession's status in society: Ekdal takes his vocation very seriously, but is subjected to fierce mockery from the other characters in the opening scene; they consider him as superficial as the images he creates. The play presents photography as a practice, as work, a profession requiring expertise and tools: in the stage directions, the time and care required for a photograph are set out; some scenes are set in the environment of a professional photographic studio, and Act III begins with Hedvig and Gina clearing up after a photograph has been taken. In addition to this emphasis on the requisite toil and mess of photographing, there is, coming from the stage directions as much as from comments by characters, a sense that this is a rather creepy form of work. The directions demand the presence onstage of the sinister tools of the photographer's trade, perhaps specifically referring to the head clamps that portrait photographers used to still their sitters, which are reminiscent of torture implements. In a letter written two years after the play's first production, in 1897, Sigmund Freud suggests these devices might prompt latent hysteria responses to childhood abuse: 'Later reluctance at photographer's, who holds the head in a clamp' (*The Complete Letters of Sigmund Freud to Wilhelm Fliess, 1887–1904*, 1985).

If the sitter is tortured and traumatised in the studio, the likeness produced is also subject to the photographer's will: in Act IV, Gina is retouching photographs, painting onto the surface of the image. Far from representing a pure form of truth, in *The Wild Duck*, photographs are posited as deceitful; the photographic studio, perhaps like the stage, or indeed the domestic sphere, is a site of the production of images that are potent but cannot be trusted. Photography provides Ibsen the opportunity to set out, to stage, some of the possibilities and problems of theatre itself. George Bernard Shaw, in his 'Appendix to *The Quintessence of*

Ibsenism' (1891), suggests that '[t]he whole point of an Ibsen play lies in the exposure of the very conventions upon which are based those by which the actor is ridden'. Shaw speculates that a bad portrayal of one of Ibsen's complex and contradictory characters (he is specifically suggesting that English actors fall short in this respect) would be like photographic retouching, 'which has made shop window photography the most worthless of the arts' (p. 198).

Photography as a discourse, in all its ambiguity, seems mapped onto a recurring stage picture in *The Wild Duck*, which the character Gregers Werle describes as 'a tableau of filial affection', created onstage, a pose suggesting that the happiness and decency of the Ekdals is pure appearance (perhaps not unlike that of the Birlings). This device influenced Anton Chekhov's *Three Sisters* (Moscow Arts Theatre, 1901), in which the posing for a photograph (by the amateur photographer and sub-lieutenant Fedotik) is a motif, a reminder of the deceptiveness with which groups and families present themselves, and Fedotik's entire collection of images is destroyed by fire in Act III, confirming the fragility of the likenesses photography is apt to produce. The relationship between realism, naturalism, and photography will be explored further in Part Three, which focuses on Bertolt Brecht.

Photographic material: *The Seven Streams of the River Ota*

Robert Lepage and Ex Machina's play *The Seven Streams of the River Ota* (Edinburgh International Festival, 1994, subsequent versions 1994–96), like *The Wild Duck*, features photographers (professional and amateur) as central characters; the act of photographing takes place at several points, and a number of photographic images feature as props or onstage projections. But the relationship with photography extends beyond the play's characters, objects, scenography, and even its themes: photography is the play's fulcrum, playfully providing its central motif, and even its unifying logic. A photographic logic is evident even in the structure of the piece, which is a discontinuous sequence of seven tableaux, each subdivided into further tableaux. The play concerns the bombing of Hiroshima, and proceeds by way of scenes taking place across five decades. As in *Three Sisters*, a set of photographs is destroyed (or 'half-destroyed') by fire, which is presented as a double of the devastation of the bomb.

Here, again, the photograph is charged with the task of supplying evidence. In the opening scene, Luke O'Connor appears, a photographer employed by the army to photograph housing and land as part of an assessment of the damage caused by the bomb. Photography supplements, and even supplies, memory, too, with capacities beyond those of the characters for remembering and narrativising; as such it is charged with attesting to or revising personal and political history. In one scene in the play, two characters named Jeffrey (part of the photographic doubling) develop photographs together, with Jeffrey 2 teaching Jeffrey 1 darkroom techniques. Together they uncover a photograph taken by Jeffrey 1's father. A later scene exploits the theatricality of the slow emergence of an image in the darkroom as a photograph is developed. The play posits photography as a way of negotiating memory, and the identity that memory constitutes: photographs echo the way in which memory can fade, or memories can be buried among other objects, but they also offer a possible strategy for establishing a sequence of events that are themselves discontinuous (or missing) fragments, or for restoring truth.

The piece seems to play on the shared terrain of theatre and photography: theatre requires that spectators be present and it insists on a continuity, even where its scenes, or tableaux, are disordered; photography takes images out of context, placing them in another configuration or confrontation elsewhere, with the possibility that a photograph might find its place anywhere. The first sequence of the play, entitled 'Moving Pictures', is particularly photographic in its form: a screen is painted and also hosts projections and silhouettes; later in the piece, still images become moving ones, and an image goes from being a material (and contingent, fire-damaged) object to appearing on a screen, before it is dragged like a computer desktop icon back into being an object again.

The Seven Streams of the River Ota plays on this emergence of movement from stillness, and of stillness from movement, and stages photographic stillness as theatrical pose: 'As the light flashes, she throws up her hand to protect her face; her image freezes' (p. 75) The scene from which this stage direction is taken is one of several happening at a photo-booth and is structured as a series of images. At the end of the sequence, the two characters wait for the strip of photographs to appear, but before the machine has finished its process of developing and printing, their train is announced and they leave. The directions state: 'A few seconds later, the pictures drop into the slot of the booth.' The distance between the taking of the image and that image's appearance echoes the characters and situations of the play, signalling to one another across time.

The use of screens and silhouettes throughout the piece exposes the play's concern with light and darkness. As in *The Octoroon*, the play of light and dark, which map onto presence and absence, recalls a shared procedure of photography and theatre, one that has been pertinent at least to theatre since the development of stage lighting, and particularly electric lighting, which came into use in the late nineteenth century. Herbert Blau, in a 1995 article entitled 'Flat-Out Vision', begins his reflections by noting that his experience of looking at photographs is shaped by the repeated experience – as a stage director as well as a theatre scholar – of sitting in the dark in theatres; Blau focuses on the shift from light to darkness of a blackout (p. 245). Lepage's play seems to employ a modality uniting the stage, the photograph, and the human eye: a photographic figuring of the optical system, whereby the trace, the outline that has been made out of light, persists on the retina upon blackout like a photograph or a negative. Explosion and exposure are fused, with the flash of the bomb as the ultimate photograph. There are blackouts indicated in the directions, not only between scenes (which corresponds to a familiar stage convention) but also between moving or still tableaux within the scenes to mark the end of one tableau and the start of another, creating a dramaturgy that recalls a strip of photographic or cinema film. Neal Ascherson's review of the Edinburgh Festival version of the play (*Independent*, 16 October 1994) describes the bomb itself in specifically photographic terms, comparing the blast of energy from a nuclear explosion to the process of photography:

> The great flash in the Hiroshima sky, by which a city was illuminated and then instantly eradicated, is also the flashbulb of the photo-booth in which people freeze their own desires and use an image to obliterate their old identities.

This points to photography's materiality, linking it to the reported phenomenon in the aftermath of Hiroshima whereby, as described in a celebrated article by John Hersey published in the *New Yorker* on 31 August 1946, 'the bomb had, in some places, left prints of the shadows that had been cast of its light' (p. 52): reportedly, human forms were burned into the walls of buildings. The nuclear blast leaves behind a trace; like a photograph it is the material result of the effect of radiation.

part two: theatre photography

Where the previous part was concerned with how photography has appeared in theatre, this one is concerned with how theatre has appeared in photographs. The question of what a theatre photograph is 'of' (and what is entailed in the 'of' of photography) imposes itself throughout. The notion of 'theatre photography' presented here is wide, and necessarily so, with the term shifting over time and referring to divergent practices of production and use. As in the previous part, the approach will be more or less chronological, but the identification of a progression in terms of photography's technological development (shifts in the mechanics and the apparatuses involved, revisions to the formulas of chemicals and the materials involved, and so on) is not an appeal to the decisive nature of technological progress. Photography's technological history might, in part, be one of scientific developments creating new possibilities, but equally must be seen as one of technology emerging in response to societal discourses, needs, and desires. And practices do not conveniently limit themselves to particular periods or places, although function and circulation may change (for example, actor 'headshots', which resemble the actor portraits discussed in the next section, are still produced today, but their circulation tends now to be limited to professional promotional contexts). The multiple practices involved in theatre photography offer a vantage point from which to consider both photography and theatre.

An article appearing on the *Guardian* blog, from 26 November 2009, deplores 'The Sorry State of Stage Photography', and addresses the complexity of theatre photography. The author, Andrew Haydon, is unimpressed with the bulk of theatre images in circulation, and in particular notes a tendency towards stage images that constitute simplifications, selections from a bigger picture, and that fail to convey 'what the production looks like'. Describing these images, primarily forms of portraiture, the author suggests that while they may be aesthetically pleasing, they do not resemble what an audience would see, and he calls for photographers to consider taking images of the entire stage, despite the technical challenges involved (in terms of detail and of scale and of scope) inherent in the making of one still image to represent a whole work. Haydon indicates a problem with the photographing of works proposing different levels of reality. The example given is a 2009 National Theatre production. Haydon argues that a photograph of *The Habit of Art*, with its play-within-a-play, would likely fall short of capturing the view of the audience (who see a small set within a large set). This would be problematic for a photographer tasked with photographing 'accurately', and a photograph would likely miss the point. The article insists on the theatre photograph's duty to render a likeness of the performance. But while this concern is shared across much of the production and reception of theatre photography, a review of historical instances of theatre photography suggests that the intentions behind theatre photographies' practices are various. Throughout, however, it is useful to note a tension between the construction of an emblematic image and the accurate rendering of an event.

Actor portraits

Joseph Donohue, a theatre historian writing about 'Evidence and Documentation' in 1989, uses the example of nineteenth-century actor portraits to discuss the dangers of reading such photographs as documenting theatre, stressing the need for supplementary information. Donohue points out a risk of anachronistic (and simply wrongheaded) viewing of a photograph informed by a particular understanding of the impetus behind photographing that is at odds with the historical practice and technical history of which the photograph is a part, and that ignores this historical practice in favour of an – entirely contemporary – zeal for documentation:

> [I]n the early days of commercial photography, in the late nineteenth century, theatrical photographers (such as Alfred Ellis, who had a studio in Baker Street) used stock backgrounds for

photographing characters in scenes from plays. A scholar unaware of this fact who thought that the photographs were taken on stage could misinterpret these background scenes as representing the actual scenery of the play, with catastrophic effects on the analysis of the mise-en-scène. (pp. 193–94)

Donohue emphasises the need for background knowledge (as well as for argument rather than the simple presentation of evidence) in scholarship, and the passage raises a question about photography's capacity to represent theatre.

A 2002 article by David Mayer in *Theatre Survey* begins with a provocative statement, which it then nuances: 'Photographs show what performers actually look like' (p. 223). Mayer explores the ways in which photographs appeal to the theatre historian, and seem to offer themselves as a solution to the very problem of being a theatre historian, allowing the viewer to be promoted to 'scientific observer' (p. 223). Mayer's engagement with photography in his opening paragraphs is a familiar one, since numerous commentators have similarly found themselves, despite an awareness of both photography's social construction and its capacity to harbour trickery, taken in by the photograph and its claim to offer up something credible: 'we tend to snatch at theatrical photographs, leaving our critical faculties at home' (p. 224). Mayer (his article is specifically about Victorian British and American actor portraits) claims that although some of these images show a 'simulation' (p. 228) of performance, they cannot simply be taken as 'evidence' in relation to a performance.

The first actor portraits were not taken in theatres, and indeed could not have been: early photographic devices were laborious to set up, and, being bulky, heavy, and also often fragile, were far from portable; the exposure time required for an image to register on early photosensitive materials was often several minutes, meaning that a clear image could be made only with an immobile camera photographing something immobile. Early photographs of people required the 'sitter' to keep very still during long exposures, and thus portraiture was initially a practice limited to the controllable environment of a space devoted to photography – the photographic studio. There are many late nineteenth-century photographs that appear to show actors performing onstage, but almost all these images are in fact studio portraits of the actors. Rather than – as, according to Donohue, might be tempting – viewing such images as attempts at capturing a performance (or imagining that such images are instances of the recording of theatre that are obliged for technical reasons to take place in a studio), we might consider them in terms of an emerging focus upon the construction of an image of an individual, playing a role within society. Actor portraits of this period are examples of a photographic trend whereby photographer and sitter devised a pose befitting the sitter's social or civic status and identity. Clothing was chosen as costume, and objects, held by the sitter or otherwise strategically placed in the image, usually pointed to a subject learning and worldliness, and often represented a particular profession (a portrait of a ship's captain might feature a sextant, for example). Naming the genre 'fiction photography', Fredric Jameson, in his 1992 *Signatures of the Visible*, calls these portraits '"realistic", insofar as it remains a historical fact that nineteenth-century bourgeois people did put on costumes to pose for such tableaux' (pp. 262–63). Indeed, studio photography enabled likenesses to be created more quickly and cheaply than had painting, and the petite bourgeoisie could thus enjoy 'a privilege hitherto reserved for the aristocracy and the well-to-do upper middle class', as Siegfried Kracauer puts it in his *Theory of Film* (1960, p. 6). The use of professional signifiers to craft an image demonstrates how sitters saw themselves, and sought to perform themselves, as members of an emerging class, but is by no means limited to late nineteenth-century photographs. The use of objects to convey profession and attendant social value forms part of an enduring sub-genre of portraiture and is present in numerous cultural representations. Images of doctors posing with stethoscopes, for example, endure, and the practice finds a concise expression in a fantasy sequence from Woody Allen's 1980 film *Stardust Memories*: trying to calm an angry monster, a character steps forward and says, 'I'm a psychoanalyst: here is my pipe.' Groucho Marx, writing for *Variety* in 1940 ('Night Life of the Gods'), pours scorn on the conventions of (movie) actor portraits, noting that all 'starlets' seem required to pose with a tennis racket at some point, ideally caught peeping through its strings.

The actor in such nineteenth-century photography is portrayed as one professional among others. Portraits of actors show the actor playing a character, sometimes with elements of stage scenery; the actor sitting – or standing – for a portrait adopted a pose for the camera, using costume and props, the tools of their particular trade. There are connections with actual stage practice: scenery might be sourced from theatres. One account, by Chantal Meyer-Plantureux, in her 'Sarah Bernhardt révélé par la photographie' from 2000, states that the nineteenth-century actress Sarah Bernhardt (the subject of a huge volume of photographs, and perhaps the most photographed person of her age) sat for a portrait in Nadar's studio surrounded by scenery and items she had borrowed for this purpose from the Odéon theatre (pp. 126–27). Actors posing in role adopted gestures as well, and these too might be 'borrowed' from performances: Lawrence Senelick, in an article about 'Melodramatic Gesture in Carte-de-Visite Photographs' (1987), points out that the project of photographer and actor (undertaken for mutual gain) was not concerned with the faithful (or otherwise) recording of a theatre performance. Actors sometimes appeared in roles they never actually played onstage, or the image might be a kind of composite, assembling borrowed elements of scenery, costume, and gesture from different roles and plays. Mayer points out that even with awareness of all the borrowing and the constructedness of the image, the scholar can nevertheless 'learn something about the actor's stance or attitude, or balance and distribution of weight' ('Quote the Words', p. 228), and that the gestures photographed – albeit limited to those that the actor would be able to sustain for the long exposure time – may be useful in developing an understanding of theatre performance.

These constructions created in the studio result in a still image, but conceiving of the photograph as still, in contrast to moving stage performance (perhaps like a still from a film), might be problematic. Senelick, addressing 'Early Photographic Attempts to Record Performance Sequence' in 1997, writes:

> Photography depended on carefully maintained poses, and, so far as acting goes, the relatively long time in which the pose had to be held was no obstacle to reproducing the theatrical moment. A pre-modern performance was a series of poses and gestures intended to stimulate a given impression. (p. 256)

This account of theatre as a sequence of held poses and gestures comes from a pre-photographic description, by Samuel Taylor Coleridge in the first volume of his *Table Talk* (1835), of watching the actor Edmund Kean: 'like reading Shakespeare by flashes of lightning' (p. 24). The actor portrait, although not taken in a theatre, not only borrows from theatre's repertoire of signs, but also seems to share its modes of delivery.

Photography participated not only in the creation of a body of theatre images, but also in their distribution. Mayer describes the circulation of actor portraits, which changed with the development of technologies and the shifts in the cost of producing photographs, and the ways in which print-ing increased the potential number of viewers of a photograph ('Quote the Words', p. 229). He describes actors' own efforts to distribute their image by way of the photograph (in concert with printing and rail technologies). For theatre personali-ties, photography provided access to a much broader audience than those who attended the theatre on any given night, and indeed could expand their reach to those who might never even go to the theatre. These images could circulate beyond the parameters of theatre spectatorship, and become emblems for individual worship: buyable, collectable, ownable images, fostering fascination for the figure of the celebrity actor.

Platonic love of theatre: a case study from Marcel Proust

It is worth citing an example, albeit one drawn from fic-tion, of the use of actor portraits by a nineteenth-century theatre spectator, an example that demonstrates the idea of theatre circulating by way of photography, and affirms how such images cannot be seen as mere reflections or shadows of events on a stage. In Proust's novel *Remembrance of Things Past* (1981, originally published in 1913), the young protag-onist, Marcel, is obsessed with plays and players; he yearns for theatre, and his desire is particularly focused on the actress Berma, who, it has been suggested, is a thinly dis-guised Bernhardt, although elsewhere in the novel, Berma's name appears in a list that also features Bernhardt's, and the character was perhaps equally inspired by actress Gabrielle Réjane, whose photographs Proust collected. Marcel considers Berma the greatest actress. Despite his enthusiasm and longing, we learn that Marcel has not yet experienced seeing (or, to use the contemporary term, hearing) Berma onstage. Young Marcel has been forbidden from actually going to the theatre (in a childhood marked by the pangs of permission and sanction), and his desire for Berma and her theatre is unconsummated – the narrator at one point calls his love for theatre 'Platonic', centred on posters on advertising columns. Eventually, permission is granted, and Marcel attends a matinee performance by Berma. But he finds himself very disappointed (pp. 480–85): Marcel is surprised at the many frustrations and distractions involved in theatregoing, and is even underwhelmed by Berma's performance. Crucially, for Marcel, attending a show seems to pale in comparison with the experience of looking at photographs of the actress, something we know he has done a great deal. As if to banish from his mind the performance he has attended, Marcel purchases a photograph of Berma after the theatre visit. That evening, he gazes at the photograph repeatedly, relighting his candle 'to look at her face once more' (p. 527). This scene of photographic viewing is prefigured in the novel when a younger Marcel imagines what watching a play might actually be like: he describes his fantasy of spectating with reference to a device, popular at the time, that permitted a photographic image to appear to the viewer as if in three dimensions:

> I almost believed that each of the spectators
> looked, as if through a stereoscope, at a scene

that existed for him alone, though similar to the thousand other scenes presented to the rest of the audience individually. (p. 79)

This ideal of a theatre experienced individually seems to disturb him even during the play. Even as he watches Berma perform, a troubled Marcel seeks 'to arrest, to immobilise' the performer before him (p. 484), and is frustrated. Things improve slightly when Berma holds a pose, 'motionless for a moment', but only until the audience applauds, breaking a 'tableau' that Marcel 'should have liked to study' (p. 484). The clapping proves that the scene does not exist for him alone, and Berma seems out of his grasp. Photography has, for Marcel, offered the promise of a kind of viewing that turns out to be unavailable at the theatre: the public experience of a play cannot (at least at this point in the story) compare to the pleasures of viewing individually and in private.

This account might offer insights for a consideration of the relationship between theatre and photography in terms of the interplay of desires and modes of looking, and, while a reader of Proust's novel knows Marcel to be a voyeuristic, sickly, and troubled youth, it is worth taking seriously the preference he expresses: photographic viewing, for Marcel, offers significant advantages over theatregoing, and, where it generates longing and desire, seems to satisfy these, or sublimate them, by way of its stillness and possibilities for repetition and control, comparing favourably with the shifting, messy, and compromised experience of a play.

From the photo session to documentary photography

Photographing actors onstage initially involved the setting up of scenes for the camera. In one of the few books devoted to the subject of theatre photography, *La Photographie du théâtre ou la mémoire de l'éphémère* (1992), Meyer-Plantureux makes a firm distinction between theatre photography from before and after 1945 that hinges on the difference between setup shots and ones that capture action. (It is the later photography that is the main subject of the book, which is in part a call for theatre photography to proliferate, but also to be taken seriously as an archive of stage practice, rather than merely satisfying commercial imperatives – which can also be mapped onto the shift she proposes.) In her discussion of pre-1945 photography, the author recounts how frozen scenes were placed onstage to be photographed. For Meyer-Plantureux, this practice, the '*séance photo*', which translates as the 'photo call' or 'photo session' (terms used more generally in the context of the press), is a direct descendant of the nineteenth-century actor portrait, substituting the stage for the studio: she compares the practice of the photo call to having the actors pose for a portrait, with the photographer cast as an artist drawing inspiration from stage action, crafting a pleasing image. Such photography, she suggests, is ultimately a disservice to the theatre work, since the photographs, however beautiful and self-contained, will have little in common with the experience of seeing the show, which she claims should be the concern of theatre photography.

Photographs belonging to this genre tend to be full-body portraits of an actor or grouping, and might even – like the actor portraits – be the result of scenes prepared exclusively for the session, with actors in configurations that never occur in the play, or two characters 'meeting' where the plot keeps them separate, with little attention paid to the stage lighting or scenery. Moreover, the angle might not be one ever seen by an audience member, and the posing actors might look at the camera (while remaining physically within a scene). Sontag suggests in her *On Photography* that 'nobody takes the same picture of the same thing' (p. 77), but the rigours and restrictions of the photo call offered a very limited range of possible images: sessions were often attended by a pack of photographers, and Meyer-Plantureux highlights the rigidity of the setup by reproducing in her book two almost identical images (of Jean-Louis Barrault and Madeleine Renaud in *Les Fausses Confidences*) taken by two different photographers (Lipnitzki and Bernand) in 1946 (p. 21). Stillness was a technical necessity for the image to register (and stage lighting was often turned up or supplemented by photographic lights on the frozen figures), but the photo call cannot be understood purely in terms of technical necessity; its enduring use even with the development of faster optics and photosensitive materials (that is, after it ceased to be the only way to obtain stage photographs) points to an aesthetic and ideological basis to the approach – identifying a particular understanding of the role of the photograph in relation to theatre, one that has been challenged by commentators from subsequent periods.

An account from the 1950s talks about 'midnight sessions' – photo calls so named because they took place immediately after a dress run: Tom Prideaux's *World Theatre in Pictures* (1953) describes photo sessions as the last straw, an unwelcome additional demand on actors who have already performed the dress (traditionally a very tense and troubled point in a production's trajectory, the point at which problems suddenly become apparent), with all of its mishaps and stoppages. Such sessions are described in harrowing terms, with the photographer characterised as an intruder arriving into a tense space of pre-first-night nerves and sudden awareness of the production's technical or artistic shortcomings, a mysterious and troublesome figure, bringing lighting that must be set up and then rearranged for each shot, sometimes earning the animosity of stagehands. The actors were required, Prideaux suggests, to submit an additional performance for the camera. He writes about the use of flash, with its blasts of light 'accompanied by a faint but sinister pop' (p. 13), and describes how one drunken actress (driven to drink, it is implied, by the 'long ordeal of rehearsals') is surprisingly able to summon up a performance, reactivated by the camera as it takes each shot: 'Whenever the camera clicked, she jumped back into her grim role, and the pictures turned out magnificently' (p. 13). Prideaux finds the elaborate apparatuses involved to be rather cumbersome and dilatory: photographers, burdened with the tools of their trade, operate too slowly or out of sync, and actually miss the best shots. He seems keen for photography to capture theatre performance as an event, rather than asserting its own logic and limitations upon it.

Another, more scholarly account, published three years later in a 1956 issue of *Revue d'histoire du théâtre*, also emphasises the laborious nature of the photo call, its demand for a supplementary show for camera after a long schedule of rehearsals. The writer, René-Thomas Coèle, considers that – despite the extra work required of the actors – the process, in the hands of a good photographer, might be worthwhile, since the resulting photographs might determine, or at least regulate, the way in which theatre is archived and remembered, thus seeming to find possibilities for the documentation of theatre in the posed photo call. Describing the work of one particular photographer, Coèle suggests that the unnecessary or modish aspects of a production are sometimes eliminated by the camera, which can enable the capturing of something essential. In this way, he suggests, the staged photograph's partiality might be redemptive, preserving the vital and eradicating all that is superficial. Photographer John Vickers (who also provided rehearsal photographs for J. B. Priestley's 1947 book *Theatre Outlook*, a rare example of published rehearsal images), writing about 'Theatre Photography' in the journal *Tabs*, defends the photo call (a practice perhaps thought to be on the way out at the time of writing – 1960), favouring it over the possible harmfulness of photographing during a run, noting that a photographer 'who *insists* on taking his pictures during the action of a play' (p. 24) – or who was unable to persuade the director to set aside time for a dedicated session – should at least have the decency to operate during a dress rehearsal. If Vickers sees photographing outside the context of a photo call as a distraction to the company, later writers, who do not necessarily share Vickers' concerns, point to the usefulness of photo calls. This is the case in theatre photographer Gerry Goodstein's 1987 article for the journal *Theatre*. For Goodstein, the photo session is not troubling; he presents it simply as a method by which the subject is optimised for the camera, angles tweaked and positions shifted, adjustments made to facilitate the creation of an engaging image, with the implication that photographs produced in this way can constitute a faithful recording (albeit one that is enhanced or adjusted). Michele Pearce, writing in 1994 in the journal *American Theatre*, favours compromise, describing calls as a necessary evil, a security measure in case photographs taken during a run or performance fail; she outlines technical challenges inherent in photographing action onstage and the possibility of missing a particular shot associated with shooting live.

Meyer-Plantureux claims that 1945 marks a turn away from photographic practices concerned with the promotion of actors or the production of press material towards the archiving of theatre productions, perhaps in the face of a conception of theatre's ephemerality (the word used in the title of her book). The shift from studio actor portraits to photo sessions can be mapped, for Meyer-Plantureux, onto a shift in theatre production: from a theatre culture and industry based on the figure of the actor-manager (who is the focus) to the advent of the figure of the theatre director (who calls the shots, arranging actors into a formation, expressing a vision). The post-1945 photography she identifies as a radical break with the previous approaches (which continue, but not without controversy, as witnessed in the above accounts) perhaps suggests a mode of photography apt to support a conception of the theatre company as a collective (headed by a director), and photographing selections from a whole posits the show as an event.

If the turning point in theatre photography for Meyer-Plantureux is 1945, then the embodiment of this shift is photographer Roger Pic, whose approach is described as the very opposite of the photo session. Pic photographed during a run of the play without using additional light, and without stoppages. Comparing Pic's photographs of the same 1946 production of *Les Fausses Confidences* with the two agency images previously mentioned, the author notes that in Pic's images the actors are no longer looking at the camera, and thus that the perspective of the camera or photographer is no longer privileged, and is no longer competing with, or attempting to supplant, the play's own representational organisation (pp. 22–26). Where the photographer's position was previously central, Pic becomes just one spectator of the show (albeit one apparently not confined to a seat), unable (and unwilling) to control or order the fleeting events of the stage. Meyer-Plantureux describes this shift as a move towards the practice of 'reportage' and the production of the 'photo-document' within theatre photography.

These terms point to a broader movement within photography whereby photographs take on the task of capturing a world in motion, and the photographer is characterised as mobile and intrepid. Such a documentarist reading of theatre photography does seem to risk a certain absurdity: one might find perverse the insistence of photographers on avoiding staging things for the camera, since, after all, what is being photographed is itself already staged. But key to Pic's waiving of previously enjoyed photographic privilege, operating without influencing and without demanding to be seen, is an attempt to approach stage action as an event. This summons a set of understandings about photography both present in many habitual ideas and articulated in critical theorisations, and perhaps acquiring additional complexity in the case of theatre photography.

Semiologist Roland Barthes tackles photography in his study of the functioning and operations of signs, drawing at various points on a photograph's particular link to a 'signified' or 'referent'. In a highly influential essay from 1961 entitled 'The Photographic Message' (which takes press photography as its starting point), published in English in *Image Music Text* (1977), Barthes identifies the photograph's particular mode of signification, distinguishing it from other forms (such as theatre), as its being a 'message without a code' (p. 17), a non-analogous image (although this idea is sometimes taken simplistically to suggest photographs are entirely neutral conveyers of the real, which is not Barthes' claim). Barthes somewhat revises his perspectives on photography in his final book (his only book on the subject of photography), *Camera Lucida* (1984, first published in 1980), in which he describes photography as 'a kind of primitive theater, a kind of Tableau Vivant' (p. 32), but still points to photography's possession of a 'that-has-been', and to the idea that it conveys something that was necessarily and undeniably 'there' (p. 76).

Sontag concludes *On Photography* with an anthology of quotations, including one from *Roget's Thesaurus*: a list of 'fields of photography', an itemisation of kinds of photography (infrared photography, candid photography, radiophotography, chronophotography, etc.). Drawing from *Roget* via Sontag, one might determine two broad ways in which photography is categorised: photography defined by how it is taken (as in the examples above) and photography defined by its subject (by what the photograph is 'of' – so, wedding photography, landscape photography), echoing the early Barthes' point. Sontag suggests that we expect photographs (more than, say, paintings) to supply a real likeness, and fundamentally do not deem photographs to be interpretations. She links this to the fact that photographs are a material trace, 'something directly stencilled off the real, like a footprint or death mask', and claims that if given a choice between two (hypothetical and anachronistic) images of Shakespeare, a painting by Hans Holbein or a photograph, Shakespeare fans would choose the photograph, since this would show how he really looked (p. 120). But stage photographs seem potentially problematic here, since they are images of something that is itself an image; theatre photography (the term does not appear in the list Sontag quotes) might require a nuancing of any understanding of photography as a direct conveyer of something (to quote Barthes again) 'that-has-been'. The notion of photography's intrinsic capacity to render likeness can be challenged with recourse to the specificity of the production of documentary images and some of the inherent contradictions of the documentary approach.

Steve Edwards, in *Photography: A Very Short Introduction* (2006), notes a discourse around documentary photography in which the photograph is posited as 'an objective, unmediated record of facts' offering 'direct access to truth'; documentary photography emphasises content rather than its form (p. 27). This results in a set of formal codes which characterise most instances of documentary photography and the approach behind them – 'no colour (black and white); no cropping; no retouching; no posing, staging or introducing extraneous objects; no additional lighting or dramatic light effects' (p. 27) – and documentary photography, despite its claims to objectivity, emerges as 'an aesthetic mode or a style' (p. 28). While discourses around documentary photography have relevance for the conception of photography more generally, and challenge the idea of a photograph as objective, Edwards avoids any assertion that photographs cannot reveal things; indeed, he challenges certain postmodern claims that photography merely 'constructs' reality, specifically with reference to the images by American military personnel of Iraqi prisoners held at Abu Ghraib prison (p. 115). These photos brought the existence and extent of the torture and abuse of Iraqi prisoners to public awareness, confounding the postmodern critique of photography, and restating the potential of photographs to be revelatory. The fact that the widely distributed Abu Ghraib photographs were stagings, with prisoners arranged into tableaux vivants, does not undermine their status as records of something that happened.

It is significant that Pic – heralded by Meyer-Plantureux as a pioneer of this documentary approach in theatre photography – used a Leica camera. This German brand of camera, whose first prototype appeared in 1913, but which was adopted widely two decades later, introduced the 35 mm × 24 mm film (originally used in movie cameras) that has been standard ever since (indeed, it is probably the only film format that can still be developed in non-specialist photographic labs). As recounted in Gianni Rogliatti's *Leica: The First Fifty Years* (1975), these were the first mass-produced handheld cameras, and their continuous roll of film allowed up to thirty-six shots to be taken before reloading (p. 1). From the early 1930s, Leicas used a rangefinder system that allowed precise focusing without measurement or guesswork, and a range of lenses increased the possible photographic subjects. The optics were particularly efficient, which meant that shorter shutter speeds could be selected, allowing moving subjects to be captured clearly, even when the camera was used without a tripod. Leicas were also relatively silent in operation. Indeed, this remains a feature of the brand's offerings today: digital and film Leica M cameras (the basic designs of which have changed very little since the 1950s) are still quieter than their SLR equivalents, and they are popular among photographers keen to shoot discreetly (for the Royal Wedding of 1981, news photographers covering the ceremony inside St Paul's Cathedral in London reportedly used Leicas for this reason). In a testament to the enduring cult status of these cameras, Leica enthusiasts on a number of web fora list films in which a character uses a Leica, and contributors to these pages note with disdain movie scenes (from *Blood Diamond*, *Spy Games*, and *Closer*, for example) in which the subtle 'click' of the Leica (the result of precise machining and the absence of a moving mirror in the design) is replaced in post-production by the more recognisable 'clunk' of an SLR mechanism. All of the Leica's features – that it is self-contained, portable, discreet, and able to capture images without additional lighting – contributed to the rise of documentary photography in the mid-twentieth century. Moreover, the Leica viewfinder, which contains a frame indicating the limits of the image, rather than – as with most contemporary cameras – being the same crop as the eventual photograph, directly posits a conception of the photograph as a selection from a wider view. Leica cameras are associated in particular with Henri Cartier-Bresson (1908–2004) and other photographers from his Magnum Photo agency, who collectively are seen as the founders of modern photojournalism. Cartier-Bresson embodied the image of the roving, voyaging photographer, and was renowned for his apparent ability to be in the right place at the right time, capturing world news events as well as remarkable scenes from everyday life (he is known as a key 'street photographer'). Despite his associations with documentary photography, however, Cartier-Bresson, in his essay 'The Decisive Moment', first published in 1952, describes himself as making images of 'the whole essence of some situation that was in the process of unroll-ing itself' (p. 23) David Bate, in his *Photography: The Key Concepts* (2009), points out that Cartier-Bresson's 'decisive moment' 'fuses a notion of instantaneity in photography (the freezing of an instant) with an older concept from art history: story-telling with a single picture' (p. 56).

Meyer-Plantureux, writing about work emerging in the middle of the twentieth century, asserts the value of pho-tography that is accurate in recording theatre, as opposed to the previous practices revolving around staged shots. While the objectivity or neutrality of such work can be challenged, it is distinct from the photo call in privileging the capturing, and indeed the preservation, of theatre as a specific event, or indeed as a performance.

Performance documentation

The notion of 'performance documentation' gained cur-rency during the second half of the twentieth century. In this domain, too, one can note a tension between captur-ing and constructing. A document on the PARIP website, dating from around 2000 and using the terminology of Baz Kershaw, delineates two kinds of performance documen-tation: 'integral' and 'external'. Integral documentation is made up of 'the mass of heterogeneous trace materials that the practice process creates', usually meaning notes and other written material, or sketches and plans. These are traces of a 'process', and become documentation through use. External documentation, on the other hand, is about recording, and is described as a method for referencing a performance. It is described as the more problematic form of documentation, since such documents might come to 'stand in' for a performance. The context of this text is the development of 'practice-based research', and it is in part a guide for artists and researchers; documentation occupies an important place in practices that aim to articulate themselves as research (and which seek to secure or maintain funding, a decisive factor in the development of performance documentation practices in recent years). The notion of performance documentation as a necessity, but also a consciousness of its being in some way troublesome, have been articulated most robustly in the field of performance studies, as a relatively new academic discipline strives to define both its own particularity and that of the work which is its object.

Documentation can form the basis for a definition of performance. A well-known characterisation of performance as ephemeral is outlined in Peggy Phelan's influential 1993 book *Unmarked: The Politics of Performance*, and particularly in the chapter 'The Ontology of Performance', in which live performance is defined in contradistinction to recording. In terms echoed in the PARIP account, the risks (not the rewards) of documentation are emphasised (fetishising, 'standing-in', generating evidence), and documentation is described as problematic and even dangerous. Phelan suggests that attempts to record performance fail to do so, since performance is precisely that which evades being recorded: earlier in the book, Phelan suggests that if a performance becomes the object of a recording process (when it is videoed, photographed, or otherwise captured on media), the result is not a performance, but simply a document (p. 31). The characterisation of performance as fleeting in nature has been challenged, notably in Rebecca Schneider's 'Archives: Performance Remains', published in *Performance Research* in 2001. The title of her article points to its claim that performance might be understood as enduring, rather than disappearing, as well as to Jacques Derrida's *Archive Fever: A Freudian Impression*, published as a book in 1996 (based on a lecture delivered by Derrida in 1994, one year after the publication of *Unmarked* – which points to a contemporary feverish concern around the notion of the archive). The most radical challenge to Phelan's argument, particularly focused on the claims it makes about performance's relationship with technologies, is Philip Auslander's 1999 book *Liveness: Performance in a Mediatized Culture* (a second edition was published in 2008), which suggests that the discourse of performance as 'live' requires that it define itself in opposition to recording, and challenges the basis of this opposition and the distinction Phelan makes. The debate staged by these two texts has become well known, with the consequence that simplistic versions of both arguments have been elaborated at points that posit a performance-versus-technology battle, evoking a scenario worthy of a horror film, where, for its defenders, live performance represents the last vestiges of life, as the only remaining living beings fight for their lives against hordes of the media undead. A more careful account of the two works is provided in

Matthew Reason's 2006 *Documentation, Disappearance and the Representation of Live Performance* (pp. 12–15), which also considers questions of photography and documentation in two chapters.

In her 1998 book *Contract with the Skin*, Kathy O'Dell writes of the 1970s performance art that is her focus: 'For the performers, photography was an imperative, the chief record of their otherwise ephemeral performances' (p. 13). Photography has the role of preserving something that would otherwise be lost. But O'Dell goes on to point to the formal characteristics of such photography, recalling the previous discussion of documentary photography: 'photographic "documents" have a style all their own, tending more often than not toward grainy black-and-white shots taken in half-lit performance spaces' (p. 13). The suggestion is that such technical shortcomings certify documentary status, with monochrome seeming to signify, or attest to, authenticity; the imperfections and partiality of the images point to the veracity of the event photographed. Photography critic A. D. Coleman, in his 1987 piece 'Collaborations through the Lens: Photography and Performance Art', seems to suggest that these formal characteristics might be deliberately used (corresponding to what Barthes calls 'reality tricks'); he mocks a 'virtually wilful ineptitude' in the photography of performance art, which he presumes is 'a signifier of photographic innocence' (p. 2). An amateurish approach, as Coleman sees it, is a 'style', as if 'an uninformed, only marginally competent amateur photographer had stumbled upon the subjects accidentally' (p. 2). Coleman describes a zeal for documenting performance art works, and quotes David Briers, who wrote provocatively, in the catalogue for an 1986 exhibition entitled *Photography as Performance*, that

> [t]here must be some examples of Performance Art which were not recorded photographically, but not to do so has become as unthinkable as not having a photographer at one's wedding. (p. 1)

Coleman identifies a dual attitude to photographing and being photographed at play in performance art: some artists have been happy to have their work be the subject of 'photographic annotation' (p. 2), but equally many have resisted having their work be recorded altogether. What becomes apparent is perhaps the coexistence of two seemingly distinct instances of a relationship between performance art and photography, which might be expressed simply as 'documentation of performance' and 'documentation as performance' (and can be mapped, at least at points, onto the opposition between capturing and crafting already identified). Pointing to photography as a modality of performance art, Briers, in his catalogue text, describes 'two linked genres' of performance photography: one is 'photo-documentation', and the other concerns staged performances, photographs of which, rather than being records of live events, are effectively art objects and performances in their own right (p. 45), and which Briers traces to the work of 'early art photographers who set up tableaux in the style of academic painters' (p. 46). The kinds of work invoked by

Briers' second genre feature heavily in Phelan's book (for example, the performative self-portraits of Cindy Sherman); Phelan's resistance to recordings of live performances is predicated on their secondary and parasitic operations.

Yves Klein's photograph 'Le Saut dans le vide' (1960), which Briers cites, and which has been a common subject of writing around performance and photography, is helpful in understanding the distinction being made. Klein's photograph shows a figure, the artist himself, falling through the air after jumping from a building, capturing him moments before he will hit the ground (a cyclist is riding away from the camera in the background). The image is not (cannot be) the documentation of a live event, since the event depicted would surely have resulted in the artist being dead (or injured), and we know that Klein did not meet such a fate in creating his work. In fact, the image is a composite of two shots (one of which shows a group of Klein's fellow judo practitioners ready to catch him; the other the street without Klein or his helpers, only the cyclist), the result of darkroom trickery. Auslander, writing in 2006 about 'The Performativity of Performance Documentation', draws on this image in describing a 'theatrical' mode of performance documentation (p. 1), which he contrasts with the 'documentary' kind tasked with recording events, and suggests that Klein's image functions by way of the fact that it '*looks* documentary' (p. 8). Auslander ends up challenging the distinction, however, with the idea that the difference between a document staging a performance and one documenting one at which an audience was present is ideological

(p. 1): 'it is not the initial presence of an audience that makes an event a work of performance art: it is its framing as performance through the performative act of documenting it as such' (p. 7); concerns about whether an audience was present (as in documentation of live events) or whether the performance was performed to the camera emphasise the wrong relationship: 'the crucial relationship is not the one between the document and the performance but the one between the document and its audience' (p. 9). This idea seems to be echoed in a discussion of works by a group of Chinese performers operating in the 1990s: in an essay from the catalogue of an exhibition, 'Action – Camera: Beijing Performance Photography' (2009), Keith Wallace states that most of the images – 'in terms of the viewer's experience of them – are the performance' rather than being 'about what took place before and after in terms of the live performance' (p. 68). Wallace discusses how performance photographs raise questions about the authorship or ownership of the photograph (identifying also how the performance's becoming or being a photograph is attended by a shift in modes and in the consequences of circulation); he notes that photographers Xing Danwen and Rong Rong have been challenged as the authors of certain of the photographs, with photographer and performer both claiming the image as their own (p. 74).

In conclusion, it is worth addressing two sets of performances and images which seem to be informed by (and to be responding to) the controversies of performance photography, and which propose nuanced tactics around the authorship of a photograph. Bock & Vincenzi's project *Invisible Dances … from Afar: A Show That Will Never Be Shown* (Arts Theatre, London, 20 March 2003) was performed once in a 'dark' theatre in the West End, with only two spectators, a 'Watcher' (Fiona Templeton, who recorded what she saw for the absent audience, who could later listen to her words by calling a dedicated telephone number) and a 'Medium' (who sought out and noted supernatural 'presences' as the show ran). Each of the work's thirty-six scenes was photographed by a camera without a photographer, the shutter of the camera staying open for the (fixed) duration of each scene. The images produced (reproduced with texts in a 2004 book) have a red cast, and are full of traces and blur, with coherent figures visible only where performers remained still long enough for their forms to register. The performance (and the book that makes up its tangible form) concerned the materiality of performance, and the performance of materiality, occupying a position where the notion of documentation falters. The photographer Manuel Vason, who has worked extensively with a range of performance artists, proposes an approach that is distinct from conventional documentation, and perhaps conceived in opposition to it (in particular in his exhibition *Encounters: Performance, Photography, Collaboration* at the Arnolfini Gallery, Bristol, in 2007). Vason works by way of 'collaboration' with artists who all create live work. The photograph does not document the artists' work in its usual instances, but is created at a given site, and rather than attempting to recreate a live performance, the process of photographing prompts the creation of an image which may, or indeed may not, correspond to the artists' live work. Vason's notion of 'collaboration' extends to the way in which his photographs are credited, with the performer's name appearing alongside the photographer's. This process seems to seek to resist the creation of a secondary photo-document, positing a performance for camera, co-created by the photographer and the photographed; as such, it is a departure from performance documentation that recalls the nineteenth-century actor portraits described above.

part three: Brecht's photography and theatre

The previous section focused on how photography has captured, recorded, or rendered theatre and performance. This part focuses on Bertolt Brecht (1898–1956), whose contradictory responses to photography (criticising its operations, but also embracing the possibilities of photography and the photographic in theatre) prepare the ground for a synthesis. Brecht will be explored from the standpoint of his theoretical claims about photography, and then in terms of his stage practice. Finally, two of Brecht's photographic projects will be examined.

In a text from around 1930 entitled 'No Insight through Photography' collected in *Bertolt Brecht on Film & Radio* (2000), Brecht describes the functioning of photography as 'the possibility of a *reproduction* that masks the context', and uses an example to highlight the problem: 'from the (carefully taken) photograph of a Ford factory no opinion about this factory can be deduced' (p. 144). Brecht attributes this insight about a photograph of a factory to Fritz Sternberg. A version of the same comment is taken up in Walter Benjamin's 1931 'Little History of Photography', with Benjamin quoting Brecht, but switching factories: 'less than ever does the mere reflection of reality reveal anything about reality. A photograph of the Krupp works or the AEG tells us next to nothing about these institutions' (p. 526). And Sontag (*On Photography*, p. 23) also indirectly quotes Brecht's point, though only the Krupp works are mentioned this time. But whichever the specific factory in question, the point (that the photograph tells us nothing) remains, and while the factories seem interchangeable, they have not been selected at random. At the time of Brecht's comment, the Ford factory was pioneering a mode of advanced industrial mass production (indeed, only a few years later, in 1934, Antonio Gramsci influentially employed the term 'Fordism' to describe it, in an analysis that resonates with Brecht's comment). Henry Ford was fervently against trade unions, contributed to anti-Semitic publications in the 1920s, and was much admired by Hitler (who is reported to have displayed a photograph of Ford in one of his offices). The German companies cited in Benjamin's version of Brecht's quotation – a steel and arms company and an electrical equipment manufacturer respectively – were both early supporters of the Führer. Brecht's point is that none of this information is conveyed by the photograph: we are none the wiser about the production taking place within the factories for seeing the photograph. Nor indeed are we any better primed for subsequent events, which Brecht is perhaps anticipating (along with Benjamin) as he writes in the very early 1930s, linking, as he does elsewhere, corporatisation and industrialisation with Hitler's project. Less than a decade after Brecht had written his text, Krupp reportedly supplied arms for the Nazis, operating a plant inside a concentration camp, just as AEG apparently produced equipment for the camps, with both companies utilising slave labour during the 1939–45 war. For Brecht, then, a photograph's dealing in mere appearances omits and even potentially conceals the social and political forces of what it portrays. And this, of course, is not a compliment, coming from Brecht.

Brecht's statement is (as evidenced in its recruitment in the other texts cited above) apt to be taken up as a concise and useful comment on the habitual operations of the photograph. As such, it is employed in attempting to define a specificity of photography, its capacity to render surface accurately. If Brecht's aesthetic and political project might be summarised as a challenge to the possibility of things appearing neutral or natural, with Brecht's various techniques seeking to undermine any such notions, then it comes as no surprise that photography, as characterised in the quotations (as manufacturing appearance), seems for Brecht to constitute a damaging and dangerous tool.

Brecht on realism, naturalism, and photography

Brecht's critique of photography seems coextensive with his critique of theatre. In the 'Appendices to the Short Organum', taken from Brecht's notes and reproduced in the 1964 collection *Brecht on Theatre: The Development of an Aesthetic*, Brecht characterises the theatre he opposes in terms that recall his comments about the photograph: 'The bourgeois theatre's performances always aim at smoothing over contradictions, at creating false harmony, at idealization' (p. 277). Such glossy theatre, like a photograph, 'teaches us nothing'. In the same document, Brecht – as elsewhere – contrasts his theatre with realist theatre, arguing against a theatre that is 'always steady', appearing to favour a theatre that – like life – proceeds 'by jerks' (p. 271), and seeming to summon photographic sequence. Brecht's views on photography, and his recourse to photography in describing theatre, can be illuminating in understanding his relationship with realism and naturalism, and they offer surprising similarities to the ideas of figures involved in the development of those forms in the late nineteenth century.

The Messingkauf Dialogues (1965) is a concise and clear elaboration of Brecht's objections to the existing theatre, and his proposals for a new one. It is, arguably, less a play than a theoretical work, or even a manifesto, and can be seen as continuing an established philosophical approach of writing in dialogue, with questions and answers, agreement and objection powering the elaboration of a philosophical position (other examples are Denis Diderot's *The Paradox of the Actor*, published posthumously in 1830; Edward Gordon Craig's 1911 *On the Art of the Theatre*, a dialogue between a Playgoer and a Stage Director; Oscar Wilde's 1891 *The Critic as Artist*; and the Socratic dialogues of Plato and Xenophon). *Messingkauf* stages a discussion, taking place over four nights, between a set of characters involved in the theatre (The Actor, The Dramaturg, The Stagehand, The Philosopher – often seen as a thinly disguised Brecht, The Actress, and The Electrician) who convene to talk and drink on a theatre stage upon which, on the first night, a set is being dismantled.

Some writings by Brecht group together 'dramatic', 'naturalistic', 'realist', and 'bourgeois' theatre (and his definition of 'Aristotelian' theatre), but *Messingkauf* offers a detailed assessment of realism and naturalism. The first section of the play is entitled 'Naturalism'. The assembled characters make clear their criticisms of realism, but they suggest that naturalism has – or at least previously had – some merit. Differentiation between these two forms can be tricky, and is inconsistent in accounts by critics and scholars: generally, naturalism is taken to be a specific development from the broader notion of realism, often defined as a historically specific style (emerging during the 1880s in the theatre) attuned – unlike realism – to setting, and to the forces, environmental and hereditary, that shape individual human existence. But such distinctions are themselves historically specific; Raymond Williams points out in a lecture from 1976:

> There is a complication here in that in the late-nineteenth century there was an attempt to distinguish realism from naturalism, and it is worth considering this distraction for a moment. In fact, naturalism, even more clearly than realism,

is not primarily defined as a dramatic or more general artistic method. Naturalism is originally the conscious opposition to supernaturalism and to metaphysical accounts of human actions, with an attempt to describe human actions in exclusively human terms with a more precise local emphasis. The relation to science, indeed consciously to natural history, the method of exhaustive analytic description of contemporary reality, and the terms naturalism and realism which have those philosophical connections, are for a time interchangeable. ('A Lecture on Realism', p. 65)

Brecht does distinguish between the terms in *Messingkauf*, but the differentiation hinges primarily on a distinction between bad and good 'realism'. The Dramaturg describes a shift whereby naturalism has morphed (or morphed back) into realism, which practice (ubiquitous at the time) The Actor describes as 'just unnatural naturalism' (p. 25). The Philosopher suggests that naturalism was in fact more realistic than the realist theatre under discussion: 'true realism', he claims, would render 'the laws that decide how the processes of life develop' (p. 27). He defines these as precisely that which 'can't be spotted by the camera', comparing Stanislavski's work to an 'image that has been mechanically drawn' (p. 24), and which cannot be interpreted, even with the aid of a magnifying glass. The Philosopher contrasts his own conception of a realistic theatre – one that goes beyond simply placing recognisable things onstage, to give access to the structural basis of situations: not merely how things are, but why they are that way – with a theatre that he finds produces 'mere photographic representations of reality' (p. 26). *Messingkauf* uses such photographic analogies to discuss – and to critique – a certain naturalism. This tactic is echoed in accounts by those involved in defining naturalism when it was emerging: August Strindberg (1849–1912), writing about Émile Zola's play *Thérèse Raquin* (Théâtre de la Renaissance, Paris, 1873, from his 1867 novel), suggests in his 1889 essay 'On Modern Drama and Modern Theatre':

> This is photography which includes everything, even the speck of dust on the camera lens; this is realism, a working method elevated to art, or the little art, which does not see the wood for the trees; this is the kind of mis-conceived Naturalism which believed that art simply consisted in copying a piece of nature in a natural way, but not the greater naturalism which seeks out those points where the great battles take place, which loves to see what one does not see every day, which delights in the struggle between natural forces, whether these forces are called love and hate, the spirit of revolt, or social instincts, which is not concerned whether something is beautiful or ugly, as long as it is great. (p. 78)

So Brecht (or his proxy, The Philosopher) and Strindberg, who might not seem like natural allies, have rather similar views on what is identified as a base form of naturalism, both favouring another naturalism that does not merely expose realistic action, settings, and events, but which renders the forces underlying them, with both using photography as an analogy to describe the less worthy, mechanical form. As with Brecht, it would be a mistake to understand this as Strindberg's being anti-photography *per se*: he was keen on photography, and in 1896 published an essay 'On the Action of Light in Photography'. Raymond Williams, in the lecture quoted above, also points to Strindberg's recruitment of the photographic:

> the terms naturalism and realism which have those philosophical connections, are for a time interchangeable, even complicated by the fact that in a famous definition Strindberg called naturalism the method which sought to go below the surface and discover essential movements and conflicts, while realism, he said, was that which reproduced everything, even the speck of dust on the lens of the camera. ('A Lecture on Realism', p. 65)

Émile Zola (1840–1902) was the first explicit advocate of the emerging movement of theatre naturalism. In the essays 'Naturalism on the Stage' (1880) and 'Naturalism in the Theatre' (1881), Zola defines theatre naturalism, a notion he brought into circulation in the years before through his novels and stories. Zola's essays are defensive, and he describes how he has been attacked by critics claiming that his use of the term 'naturalism' offers nothing, since art has always been concerned with truth. Zola counters this by suggesting that naturalism is distinct in that it constitutes a specific approach made possible by a specific set of historical conditions (he links this to the French Revolution), and he trumpets its necessity for the theatre to remain relevant.

Like many figures of the era, but perhaps with more zeal and skill than most, Zola turned his hand to photography, in the mid-1880s, reportedly as a result of having completed his cycle of novels. In the aftermath of the Dreyfus affair, which saw Zola exiled in South Norwood in London, he produced a large number of images – pictures of friends and family, but also urban landscapes: he photographed Crystal Palace, as well as, back in France, the Eiffel Tower. Zola promotes photography as a method of seeing, a scientific one – a means by which anything could be viewed and scrutinised. He linked it to the theatre he was trying to create as he called for a great theatre artist to do what Honoré de Balzac did for the novel, to complete what he called the naturalist revolution (p. 67). Zola (quoted in Sontag, *On Photography*, the quote apparently from a 1901 meeting of a Paris photography club) declares that 'you cannot claim to have really seen something until you have photographed it' (p. 67), which for Sontag amounts to evidence that, by 1901, photography had already become constitutive of reality. Georges Didi-Huberman takes up this quotation in his *Invention of Hysteria* ([1982] 2003), and finds Zola's claim to be accurate, linking this to the capacity of photography to grant access to that which the eye cannot see. Photography does this by way of its optics and its recording mechanism. The photographic lens, like a telescope (the device central to Brecht's 1945 play *Life of Galileo*), enables a viewer to see things invisible to the naked eye, allowing things to be scrutinised away from their original context.

Given his negative assessment of a photograph (it 'teaches us nothing'), it might be surprising to learn that Brecht was a collector of photographs: his work books contain photographs supplementing the text entries, and he was himself, according to Meyer-Plantureux in *La Photographie de théâtre* (p. 28), a keen and technically proficient photographer. Echoing the form of his diary and work books, Brecht undertook a major project combining photographs and text which draws on photography's ability to posit an image, but militates against 'neutral' photographic use by playing with photographs' context. For Brecht, photography must remain useless at best or suspect at worst unless it can be mobilised, and thus made to reveal the forces and social relationships at play under its surface. Only then might it teach us something.

War Primer

The decontextualisation and recontextualisation of photographic images is the ambition of Brecht's *War Primer*, published in Germany in 1955 and in Britain in 1998. The title references primer textbooks of the kind used in schools, and attests to the formal simplicity of the project – a picture book with a few lines of text – as well as to a pedagogical intent.

War Primer is a collection of images from the Second World War, gathered by Brecht over several years (each image's source is not always given in full, but most are clipped from newspapers and periodicals). In many cases, the images are reproduced complete with their original captions. As John Willett suggests in his afterword to the English-language edition, the sources map Brecht's journey as an exile during the war (in 1933 he had left Germany for Czechoslovakia; he then went on to Denmark, Sweden, and eventually the United States), and suggest continuous motion and a distanced perspective: news from the theatres of war.

In addition to collating the photographs, Brecht writes a short verse to accompany each, placed underneath it in a box. Brecht's words supplement the images; the reader must take into account two, or three (where there appears the original caption, and this prose contrasts with Brecht's verse), elements. This prompts work for the reader/viewer, who must connect image and text. With this project, Brecht is addressing his distrust of photographs, manoeuvring them to operate against their usual tendencies, and in particular is critiquing the masking of truth he has located in the photojournalistic use of images of war. A procedure of this kind – engaging sequence, and creating juxtapositions that are at times shocking or disconcerting – fits with the wider Brechtian aesthetic project. The privileging of contradiction or discontinuity can be linked to the filmic technique of montage. A key term in film theory, the word is French for 'editing', but in addition to the technical procedure of splicing and joining film, it is used to express the deliberate use of editing to create meaning by way of disparate elements. Montage figures in the list of constituents of 'epic' theatre in Brecht's 'The Modern Theatre Is the Epic Theatre' (originally part of the notes to accompany his 1930 production *Rise and Fall of the City of Mahagonny*): the list has two columns, one for the existing 'Dramatic Theatre', and one for the 'Epic Theatre' he is proposing. 'Montage' is placed in opposition to 'growth', suggesting discontinuity and sudden shifts. Montage is particularly associated with the filmmaker Sergei Eisenstein (1898–1948), although Brecht's recruitment of the technique is arguably informed just as much by the work of Charlie Chaplin (1889–1977), which he admired. In the interaction of the elements, image to image, and word to image, *War Primer* prompts a mode of reading that must skip between the elements in play on the page, a distantiated mode of reception. The realism of habitual photographic editing, the original treatment of the images used, is supplanted by montage, with the potential for access to social and political forces. *War Primer*'s process corresponds to a proposal for new 'Uses of Photography' in Berger's essay, which is concerned with the urgent task of changing our relationship with photographs. The critical mobilisation of photographs beyond their habitual uses (the earlier part of Berger's essay describes how, in the nineteenth century, the photograph enjoyed a status as the natural conveyer of appearances) echoes Brecht's approach in *War Primer*. Berger is scornful of the typical use of captions, which he describes as tautological (p. 64), and he proposes that a radical approach to contextualising an image is needed. New uses of photography, Berger suggests, might be learnt by following instructions given in a verse written by Brecht as advice to his players (the title is 'Portrayal of Past and Present in One', and Berger quotes from the second half of the poem). Brecht proposes that the actor should:

> make the instant
> Stand out, without in the process hiding
> What you are making it stand out from.
>> Give your acting
> That progression of one-thing-after-another,
>> that attitude of
> Working up what you have taken on. In this way
> You will show the flow of events and also the course
> Of your work, permitting the spectator
> To experience this Now on many levels, coming from
>> Previously and
> Merging into Afterwards, also having much else Now
> Alongside it. He is sitting not only
> In your theatre but also
> In your world. (Quoted in Berger, 'Uses of
>> Photography', p. 65)

Berger suggests that Brecht's term 'instant' might be mapped onto 'photography', and 'acting' onto 'the recreating of context' (p. 65). Berger claims that most photographs can achieve usefulness only if an 'adequate context' is created for them, and this constitutes the institution of a new narrative, and entrance into historic time. *War Primer* – which is not mentioned in Berger's essay – seems to propose just such a modality.

Photography models theatre; theatre models photography

In a 1953 entry from his working diary, Brecht notes that a set of photographs by Ruth Berlau (1906–74), a longstanding colleague, highlight problems of staging. Significantly, the comments indicate that these photographs had been taken the previous day, and thus had been developed and printed overnight (perhaps in a darkroom at the theatre, according to Meyer-Plantureux), suggesting an integral role for such photographs in the working practices of Brecht's theatre. Meyer-Plantureux quotes the diary in her introduction to a book of photographs by Pic, *Bertolt Brecht et le Berliner Ensemble à Paris* (1995), and states that photographs constituted a tool for Brecht, enabling him to pick out (and then correct) errors of blocking and of lighting (p. 28). This is supported by a comment from Brecht in his 1949 text 'Masterful Treatment of a Model' (published in English in 1964), in which he notes that the photographs show details of the actors' makeup (p. 214). This recruitment of photography as part of the rehearsal and production process, while not unique, was – and remains – rare, and Brecht was likely one of the first practitioners to employ photographs in this way. The practice recalls other instrumental uses of photography as a means of checking things that might escape human perception, for example in a factory (where high-speed photography is used to monitor the functioning of a machine) or in sport (the 'photo-finish').

Brecht, although critical of claims of photographic objectivity, drew nevertheless on photography's technological abilities to isolate and magnify, and to record information. Benjamin writes that the lens, unlike the eye, 'is adjustable and can easily change viewpoint' (p. 103), and he points to the resultant ability of photography to isolate temporally as well as spatially: photography's specific power to create a frozen image from a subject in motion. In this influential 1936 essay on 'The Work of Art in the Age of Its Technological Reproducibility', Benjamin writes that photography can 'bring out aspects of the original that are accessible only to the lens' (p. 103). Here, we can consider theatre as the original work of art subject to reproduction by photograph. A theatre photograph can reveal details unseen by a spectator, even a director, and prompts a circulation of the image. Benjamin defines the other key specificity of new technological forms in terms of such circulation: 'technical reproduction can place the copy of the original in situations which the original itself cannot attain' (p. 103). Brecht, in his 1932 article 'The *Threepenny* Lawsuit', writes about the development of 'apparatuses' (he is referring to theatre in such terms initially), and gives photography as an example of something that has actually declined with its technological advances. While he notes the practicality of the new equipment (its ability to shoot close-up shots, the wider tolerance of lighting conditions – features he himself makes use of, as noted above), he suggests that contemporary photographic portraits produce worse 'likenesses' than did the Daguerreotype. The reason he gives for this is that the Daguerreotype, with its 'relatively long' exposure time, would ensure that 'several expressions ended up on the plate' (p. 173). It is as if, for Brecht, a good photographic image would be a composite of images, and would materially contain the trace of movement. Brecht's point echoes (once again) one made by Benjamin, who, in his 1931 'Little History of Photography', claims that such images are more striking and alive than later photographs, and that 'during the considerable period of the exposure, the subject (as it were) grew into the picture' (p. 514). Brecht, attuned to the implications of photographic reproduction, drew on its possibilities for his work. But further Brecht sought to address the limitations he identified, and harnessed photographs in his work in an integral and systematic manner, proposing photographic sequence in the development and circulation of his theatre.

Brecht and his colleagues (principally Berlau) created *Modellbücher*, a term which can be translated as 'model-books', although some English translations of and commentaries on Brecht opt for the term 'model' (which is also used in reference to Brecht's 'model productions', which are linked to and sometimes theorised together with modelbooks). The term seems to be Brecht's, although he was probably influenced by Max Reinhardt, who had used *Regie-buch* (a file containing heterogeneous items relating to the staging of a play – a development of the more traditional, and textual, 'prompt book'). The *Modellbuch* was a large collection of sketches and photographs, along with text, from productions. Substantial modelbooks were made for numerous productions, including at least one production of *Mother Courage* (Deutsches Theater, Berlin, 1949) and *Antigone* (Stadttheater, Chur, Switzerland, 1948). Willett, in *Brecht on Theatre* (1964), states that Berlau made proto-modelbooks for stagings of *The Mother* (Borups Højskole, Copenhagen, 1935) and *Señora Carrar's Rifles* (Borups Højskole, Copenhagen, 1937), recruiting photographs from previous productions (p. 212, n.1), suggesting that the use of this modality precedes Brecht's written theorisation of it. Images were 'accompanied by explanatory instructions', as Brecht puts it in his 1949 'Masterful Treatment of a Model' (p. 211), and sections from the play's dialogue, confronting image with text, not unlike the modality of *War Primer*. According to Meyer-Plantureux, in *La Photographie du théâtre*, Brecht was at one point troubled by the technical imperfection of the images in the modelbooks, and sought the assistance of a chemist in trying to create images closer to the Daguerreotypes he admired – images that stand alone as well as participating in a series (p. 28). The modelbooks housed what Willett calls 'a complete photographic record' of a production (p. 220), but are distinct from simple documentation in that they served as a guidebook (a primer, perhaps, or indeed a 'model') for future stagings, facilitating a recreation of elements of the production. In a dialogue with E. A. Winds entitled 'Does the Use of the Model Restrict the Artist's Freedom?', Brecht explains how this approach informs his work, asserting that there is nothing shameful or slavish about copying:

> We must realise that copying is not so despicable as people think. It isn't 'the easy way out'. It's no disgrace, but an art. Or rather it needs to be developed into an art. (p. 224)

Brecht links this idea of 'copying' to the adoption (or indeed adaptation) of story employed in creating drama, averring that copying from a model is surely no worse than following stage directions. Copying, he proposes, is an art that must be learnt, and he emphasises that the models produced must be 'imitable'. But Brecht nuances this in his 'Masterful Treatment' essay from the same year: the model (Brecht refers both to a model production and to the modelbooks) is neither a new way of scripting a play nor 'a blueprint' (p. 211); it is 'not set up to fix the style of performance' (p. 212). In order to be useful, in fact, it must be 'by definition incomplete', with 'shortcomings' that 'cry out for improvement', prompting the (future) production to take up the slack (p. 212); rather than dictating the form of the production, the modelbooks might be seen as a provocation.

Brecht seems to insist, through his defence of copying but also his requirement that the photographs make demands on the theatre production through their partiality, on the possibility and necessity of an interrelation between photography and theatre. The modelbooks are made up of recordings, but these arrangements furnish instructions, an impetus for the creation of stage work. This suggests a practice in which images are mobile and interchangeable that is supported in accounts of Brecht's stage work. Benjamin – without reference to (or perhaps even awareness of) the modelbooks – observes in Brecht's epic theatre a photographic logic at play. In his 1939 essay 'What Is Epic Theatre? [Second Version]', included in *Understanding Brecht* (1998), Benjamin observes the importance of gesture in Brecht's epic theatre, and defines the epic theatre's contribution as 'Making gestures quotable': the actor in this theatre might both repeat a gesture previously made and reproduce another character's gesture at a given point (p. 19). Gestures are thus discrete and mobile, and delivered in a way that resembles the setting out (and the 'rearrangeability') of type. Benjamin proposes in his essay that this technological character, of sequence and discontinuity, of epic theatre is part of what distances it from Aristotelian theatre. Epic theatre is compared to the 'images on a film strip': it 'proceeds in fits and starts' (p. 22). Benjamin seems to invite the idea that photographs and theatre both participate in a network of signification, with images becoming exchangeable units in the work. Or some images do: in an article from 1990 entitled 'Reading Scenic Writing: Barthes, Brecht, and Theatre Photography', Jim Carmody makes an extensive study of theatre photography in Brecht's theatre, examining Brecht's use of photography in the context of his recruitment of stage images in his work (linking this to Diderot, via Brecht, and to Gotthold Ephraim Lessing and the idea of a stage tableau). While the emphasis Brecht places on creating tableau onstage images might support the idea of a theatre that operates by way of a photographic logic, Carmody is attentive to the difference between such stage images and the images made possible by photography, and points out that Brecht's tableaux themselves cannot be photographed (since the photograph would lack the stage tableau's contextual framing). In that light, it may be that what Brecht does is enable a collision, rather than a reconciliation, between these two kinds of image.

Brecht embraces both the scientific accuracy of photographs and their ability to create pictures, and posits an interpenetration of photography and theatre. The relationship proposed is not only one wherein photographs record theatre and theatre stages photographs, but one where photographing and staging change form as the two adopt each other's procedures, resulting in those procedures being transformed. As such, the modelbooks not only record or transmit Brecht's theatre, but are its continuation by other means.

Throughout his writings, Brecht seems to be haunted by film; despite a keen interest in (and sometimes enthusiasm for) cinema, his actual relationship with film production was quite troubled. Like Benjamin, Brecht saw great potential in film, despite being a fervent critic of its operations as part of the emerging mass culture in the early twentieth century; indeed, his writings are full of references to existing film as inheriting the 'bad' realism of the nineteenth-century theatre, and he often defines his theatre in contrast to it. Brecht produced barely any film work, and accounts of his film work in Germany and later in the United States are marked by frustration and defeat. The only film with which he was associated that seems to have been successful in his terms, or which was without litigation, was the 1932 German film *Kuhle Wampe*. The introduction to *Bertolt Brecht on Film & Radio* states that Hollywood cinema held a fascination for Brecht, and that he made several attempts to produce work in the burgeoning cinema industry, but that these were thwarted (pp. xi–xii). This difficult trajectory differentiates him from many of his fellow exiles in Los Angeles during the war, who were able more readily than Brecht to make the transition to commercial cinema: his participation as a writer on Fritz Lang's 1943 *Hangmen Also Die!* ended with Brecht challenging the crediting of the film to another screenwriter (echoing the copyright case Brecht had brought in 1930 against the production company of Georg Wilhelm Pabst's film version of his 1928 play *Threepenny Opera*), and many projects were planned but did not materialise. Brecht described Los Angeles as 'Hell' in a poem written during his six-year stay, and his American adventure ended with him leaving the country after being called before the House Un-American Activities Committee. Since Brecht failed to make films (or was prevented from doing so), it is not possible to know what tactics he would have employed. *Kuhle Wampe*, with its use of montage in particular, does offer more than a glimpse of the Brechtian politicisation of aesthetics. But it should be possible further to imagine what Brecht's cinema might have been by way of the interplay of photography and theatre, or even to envisage that it is in the interrelation of photography and theatre that Brecht's cinematic ambitions come closest to fruition. Film's potential for figures like Brecht and Benjamin (both contrast actually existing film with the broad possibilities the medium might allow) seems to reside in the persistence of its photographic materiality and character, and to point back to the emergence of moving pictures at the end of the nineteenth century.

The sequential aspect of the modelbooks elicits a comparison with film, and explicit reference to film (in its photographic constitution) is made in Benjamin's account of epic theatre. Both of these sequences of images present in Brecht's work point to a form based on the significance of the shift between motion and stillness. This recalls the pre- and proto-cinematic photographic practice of 'chronophotography' (literally, 'time-photography'), which mounted attempts to capture movement photographically, isolating still, sequential shots or tracking trajectories of motion. The earliest chronophotography was that undertaken by Pierre Jules César Janssen (1824–1907), who in 1874 used photographic technology he had invented to observe the Transit of Venus (the Transit is a subject of Brecht's *Life of Galileo*, which also references the proto-photographic device the *camera obscura*), but the most celebrated work is that of chronophotographers who focused on the study of human motion, particularly Étienne-Jules Marey (1830–1904) and Eadweard Muybridge (also 1830–1904). The latter is known for demonstrating how a horse gallops, step by step, by way of a photographic apparatus, and later for his sequential images of humans and animals (particularly in the

1887 publication *Animal Locomotion*). Chronophotography tests photography's ability to capture, and is scientific in its avowed aims, but subsequent accounts by critics Marta Braun (*Picturing Time*, 1992) and Linda Williams (*Hard Core*, 1989) have challenged this, at least in the work of Muybridge, and pointed to the ways in which Muybridge's images are a staging of scientific status, as well as to evidence that the images are not necessarily captured (stilled) motion, but sets of poses held for the camera.

Brecht's collision of photography and theatre, and its complex recruitment of crafted and captured images, concludes this book, with reference to cinema, which perhaps haunts any consideration of photography and theatre. Just as Brecht seems to look back to the emergence of film and the uneasy relationship between stillness and motion that attended it as a set of possibilities for theatre, it seems appropriate to close this book by considering how the interplay of stillness and motion asserts itself today. While the optical apparatus of photography has changed strikingly little since the era of Brecht, the storage apparatus has changed considerably with digital technology. The change is sometimes expressed as quantitative, in terms of the speed with which digital images appear and can circulate and participate in distribution networks, or in terms of reproducibility, whereby digital confounds notions of the original, and prompts a crisis in that its images can be manipulated easily and sometimes without trace. But digital photographing can also collapse the distinction between still and moving image, in the sense that recording equipment (cameras) and transmission devices (screens and projectors) are capable of dealing with both with minimal differentiation. But the same set of technologies can also reassert the opposition between stillness and motion: Laura Mulvey's *Death 24x a Second: Stillness and the Moving Image* (2006) considers how digital viewing technologies have impacted the viewing and study of cinema, noting a shift whereby still images, previously buried in cinematic flow, are revealed, and Mulvey links these uncovered stillnesses with cinema's other, persisting stillnesses, its tableaux and freeze-frames. It remains to be seen how the shifts prompted by digital technology will undermine or reinforce the staging and posing that takes place between theatre and photography.

further reading

Ascherson, Neal. 'Shining in the Shadow of the Two Suns: Neal Ascherson Was Seized by Robert Lepage's New Show.' *The Independent* 16 Oct. 1994.

Auslander, Philip. *Liveness: Performance in a Mediatized Culture*. London: Routledge, 1999.

———. 'The Performativity of Performance Documentation.' *Performing Arts Journal* 84 (2006): 1–10.

Barthes, Roland. *Camera Lucida: Reflections on Photography*. [1980]. Trans. Richard Howard. London: Flamingo, 1984.

———. 'The Photographic Message.' [1961]. *Image Music Text*. Ed. and trans. Stephen Heath. London: Fontana, 1977. 15–31.

Bate, David. *Photography: The Key Concepts*. Oxford: Berg, 2009.

Benjamin, Walter. 'Little History of Photography.' [1931]. Trans. Edmund Jephcott and Kingsley Shorter. *Selected Writings*. Ed. Michael W. Jennings, Howard Eiland, and Gary Smith. Vol. 2. Cambridge, MA: Belknap, 1999. 507–30.

———. 'What Is Epic Theatre? [Second Version].' [1939]. *Understanding Brecht*. Trans. Anna Bostock. London: Verso, 1998. 15–22.

———. 'The Work of Art in the Age of Its Technological Reproducibility.' [1936]. *Selected Writings: 1935–1938*. Ed. Howard Eiland and Michael W. Jennings. Vol. 3. Cambridge, MA: Belknap, 2002. 101–33.

Berger, John. 'Uses of Photography.' *About Looking*. New York: Vintage, 1980. 52–67.

Blau, Herbert. 'Flat-Out Vision.' *Fugitive Images: From Photography to Video*. Ed. Petro Patrice. Bloomington: Indiana UP, 1995. 245–64.

Bock & Vincenzi. *Invisible Dances ... from Afar: A Show That Will Never Be Shown*. London: Artsadmin, 2004.

Boucicault, Dion. *The Octoroon; or, Life in Louisiana*. [1859]. Reprint. North Stratford, NH: Ayer, 1999.

Bourdieu, Pierre. *Photography: A Middle-Brow Art*. [1965]. Cambridge: Polity, 1990.

Braun, Marta. *Picturing Time: The Work of Etienne-Jules Marey (1830–1904)*. Chicago, IL: U of Chicago P, 1992.

Brecht, Bertolt. 'Appendices to the Short Organum.' [c.1948]. *Brecht on Theatre: The Development of an Aesthetic*. Ed. and trans. John Willett. London: Methuen, 1964. 276–81.

———. *Bertolt Brecht on Film & Radio*. Ed. Marc D. Silberman. London: Methuen, 2000.

———. *Brecht on Theatre: The Development of an Aesthetic*. Ed. and trans. John Willett. London: Methuen, 1964.

———. 'Does Use of the Model Restrict the Artist's Freedom?' *Brecht on Theatre: The Development of an Aesthetic*. Ed. and trans. John Willett. London: Methuen, 1964. 222–25.

———. 'Masterful Treatment of a Model.' [1949]. *Brecht on Theatre: The Development of an Aesthetic*. Ed. and trans. John Willett. London: Methuen, 1964. 209–15.

———. *The Messingkauf Dialogues*. Trans. John Willett. London: Methuen, 1965.

———. 'The Modern Theatre Is the Epic Theatre.' [1930]. *Brecht on Theatre: The Development of an Aesthetic*. Ed. and trans. John Willett. London: Methuen, 1964. 33–42.

———. 'No Insight through Photography.' *Bertolt Brecht on Film & Radio*. Ed. Marc D. Silberman. London: Methuen, 2000. 144.

———. 'The *Threepenny* Lawsuit.' [1932]. *Bertolt Brecht on Film & Radio*. Ed. Marc D. Silberman. London: Methuen, 2000. 147–99.

———. *War Primer*. [1955]. Trans. and ed. John Willett. London: Libris, 1998.

Briers, David. 'Photography and Performance Art.' *Photography as Performance: Message through Object and Picture*, 11 September–18 October 1986. Sel. Tony Arefin and Maureen O. Paley. London: Photographers' Gallery, 1986. 43–46.

Carmody, Jim. 'Reading Scenic Writing: Barthes, Brecht, and Theatre Photography.' *Journal of Dramatic Theory and Criticism* 5.1 (1990): 25–38.

Cartier-Bresson, Henri. 'The Decisive Moment.' [1952]. *The Mind's Eye: Writings on Photography and Photographers*. New York: Aperture, 1999. 20–43.

Coèle, René-Thomas. 'Photographies de Théâtre: H. J. Mydtskov.' *Revue d'histoire du théâtre* 1 (1956): 63–64.

Coleman, A. D. 'Collaborations through the Lens: Photography and Performance Art.' *Doc-U-Men-Tia*. Ed. f-stop Fitzgerald. San Francisco, CA: Last Gasp, 1987. 1–5.

Coleridge, Samuel, and Henry Nelson Coleridge. *Specimens of the Table Talk of the Late Samuel Taylor Coleridge*. London: John Murray, 1835.

Derrida, Jacques. *Archive Fever: A Freudian Impression*. Trans. Eric Prenowitz. Chicago, IL: U of Chicago P, 1996.

Dickinson, Thomas Herbert. *An Outline of Contemporary Drama*. New York: Biblo and Tannen, 1969.

Diderot, Denis, 'Lettre à Madame Riccoboni.' *Paradoxe sur le comédien*. [1758]. Paris: Folio, 1994. 127–43.

Didi-Huberman, Georges. *Invention of Hysteria: Charcot and the Photographic Iconography of the Salpêtrière*. [1982]. Trans. Alisa Hartz. Cambridge, MA: MIT Press, 2003.

Donohue, Joseph. 'Evidence and Documentation.' *Interpreting the Theatrical Past: Essays in the Historiography of Performance*. Ed. Thomas Postlewait and Bruce A. McConachie. Iowa City: U of Iowa P, 1989. 177–97.

Eastlake, Lady Elizabeth. 'Photography.' [1857]. *Classic Essays on Photography*. Ed. Alan Trachtenberg. New Haven, CT: Leete's Island Books, 1980. 39–68.

Edwards, Steve. *Photography: A Very Short Introduction*. Oxford: Oxford UP, 2006.

Flusser, Vilém. *Towards a Philosophy of Photography*. London: Reaktion, 2000.

Franck, Martine. *One Day to the Next*. New York/Paris: Aperture/Maison européenne de la photographie/Seuil, 1998.

Freud, Sigmund. *The Complete Letters of Sigmund Freud to Wilhelm Fliess, 1887–1904*. Ed. and trans. Jeffrey Moussaieff Masson. Cambridge, MA: Belknap, 1985.

Goodstein, Gerry. 'Past, Present, Future Photography: An Essay and Photo Portfolio.' *Theatre* 18.2 (1987): 22–25.

Haydon, Andrew. 'The Sorry State of Stage Photography.' *The Guardian* Theatre Blog 26 Nov. 2009. <www.theguardian.com/stage/theatreblog/2009/nov/26/stage-theatre-photography-celebrity>.

Hersey, John. 'A Reporter at Large: Hiroshima.' *The New Yorker* 31 Aug. 1946: 15.

Holmes, Oliver Wendell. 'The Stereoscope and the Stereograph.' [1859]. *Classic Essays on Photography*. Ed. Alan Trachtenberg. New Haven, CT: Leete's Island Books, 1980. 71–82.

Jameson, Fredric. *Signatures of the Visible*. London: Routledge, 1992.

Kracauer, Siegfried. *Theory of Film: The Redemption of Physical Reality*. Princeton, NJ: Princeton UP, 1960.

Krauss, Rosalind. 'A Note on Photography and the Simulacral.' [1984]. *Over Exposed: Essays on Contemporary Photography*. Ed. Carol Squiers. New York: New Press, 1999. 169–82.

Lepage, Robert, and Ex Machina. *The Seven Streams of the River Ota*. London: Methuen, 1996.

Marx, Groucho. 'Night Life of the Gods (*Variety*, January 30, 1940).' *The Essential Groucho*. Ed. Stefan Kanfer. London: Penguin, 2000. 166–69.

Mayer, David. 'Quote the Words to Prompt the Attitudes: The Victorian Performer, the Photographer and the Photograph.' *Theatre Survey* 43.2 (2002): 223–51.

McLuhan, Marshall. *Understanding Media: The Extensions of Man*. New York: McGraw-Hill, 1964.

Meyer-Plantureux, Chantal. 'Sarah Bernhardt révélé par la photographie.' *Portrait(s) de Sarah Bernhardt*. Ed. Noëlle Guibert. Paris: Bibliothèque Nationale de France, 2000. 125–31.

———. *La Photographie de théâtre ou la mémoire de l'éphémère*. Paris: Paris Audiovisuel, 1992.

Meyer-Plantureux, Chantal, and Benno Besson. *Bertolt Brecht et le Berliner Ensemble à Paris: Photographies de Roger Pic*. Paris: Marval and Arte Editions, 1995.

Mulvey, Laura. *Death 24x a Second: Stillness and the Moving Image*. London: Reaktion, 2006

O'Dell, Kathy. *Contract with the Skin: Masochism, Performance Art, and the 1970s*. Minneapolis: U of Minnesota P, 1998.

PARIP. 'PARIP FAQs.' n.d. 5 Jun. 2003. <www.bris.ac.uk/parip/faq. htm>.

Pearce, Michele. 'In Search of the Decisive Moment: A Gallery of Theatre Photography.' *American Theatre* 11.3 (1994): 32–39.

Phelan, Peggy. *Unmarked: The Politics of Performance*. London: Routledge, 1993.

Picon-Vallin, Béatrice, ed. *Les Écrans sur la scène*. Lausanne: Age d'homme, 1998.

Prideaux, Tom. *World Theatre in Pictures*. New York: Greenberg, 1953.

Priestley, J. B. *An Inspector Calls and Other Plays*. London: Penguin, 2000.
———. *Theatre Outlook*. London: Nicholson & Watson, 1947.

Proust, Marcel. *Remembrance of Things Past*. [1913]. Trans. C. K. Scott Moncrieff and Terence Kilmartin. Vol. 1. London: Penguin, 1981.

Reason, Matthew. *Documentation, Disappearance and the Representation of Live Performance*. Houndmills, UK: Palgrave Macmillan, 2006.

Rogliatti, Gianni. *Leica: The First Fifty Years*. Hove, UK: Hove Camera Photo Books, 1975.

Sandburg, Carl. Prologue. *The Family of Man*. Comp. Edward Steichen. New York: Museum of Modern Art, 1955.

Schneider, Rebecca. 'Archives: Performance Remains.' *Performance Research* 6.2 (2001): 100–108.

Senelick, Laurence. 'Early Photographic Attempts to Record Performance Sequence.' *Theatre Research International* 22.3 (1997): 255–64.
———. 'Melodramatic Gesture in Carte-De-Visite Photographs.' *Theatre* 18.2 (1987): 5–13.

Shaw, George Bernard. 'Appendix to *The Quintessence of Ibsenism*.' [1891]. *The Theory of the Modern Stage*. Ed. Eric Bentley. Harmondsworth, UK: Penguin, 1968. 197–218.

Sontag, Susan. *On Photography*. Harmondsworth, UK: Penguin, 1977.

Strindberg, August. 'On Modern Drama and Modern Theatre.' [1889]. *Selected Essays by August Strindberg*. Ed. Michael Robinson. Cambridge: Cambridge UP, 1996. 73–86.

———. 'On the Action of Light in Photography.' [1896]. *Selected Essays by August Strindberg*. Ed. Michael Robinson. Cambridge: Cambridge UP, 1996. 160–64.

Szarkowski, John. *The Photographer's Eye*. [1966]. London: Secker & Warburg, 1980.

Tagg, John. *The Burden of Representation*. Houndmills, UK: Palgrave Macmillan, 1988.

Vason, Manuel. *Encounters: Performance, Photography, Collaboration*. Bristol, UK: Arnolfini, 2007.

Vickers, John. 'Theatre Photography.' *Tabs* 18.3 (1960): 23–28.

Wallace, Keith. 'Action – Camera: Beijing Performance Photography.' *Action – Camera: Beijing Performance Photography*. Keith Wallace, Thomas J. Berghuis, and Maya Kovskaya. Vancouver: Morris and Helen Belkin Art Gallery, 2009. 67–80.

Wertenbaker, Timberlake. *The Line*. London: Faber and Faber, 2009.

Williams, Linda. *Hard Core: Power, Pleasure, and the 'Frenzy of the Visible'*. Berkeley: U of California P, 1989.

Williams, Raymond. 'A Lecture on Realism.' *Screen* 18.1 (1976): 61–74.

Zola, Émile. '*From* Naturalism in the Theatre.' [1881]. *The Theory of the Modern Stage: An Introduction to Modern Theatre and Drama*. Ed. Eric Bentley. Harmondsworth, UK: Penguin, 1968. 351–72.

———. 'Naturalism on the Stage.' [1880]. *Dramatic Theory and Criticism: Greeks to Grotowski*. Ed. Bernard E. Dukore. New York: Holt, 1974. 692–719.

index

Printed in Great Britain
by Amazon